MODERN
GRANNY STITCH
CROCHET

Make clothes and accessories
using the granny stitch

CLAUDINE POWLEY

DAVID & CHARLES

www.davidandcharles.com

Contents

Welcome

There's a good chance you've picked this book because you've fallen in love with granny stitch and want to see what else you can do with it. Granny stitch is a fun and versatile stitch pattern that can be used in a variety of ways. It is usually one of the first stitches people learn because it's quick, easy and produces a lovely vintage look. However, it can be made to look modern if you take a fresh approach to the colours and patterns used.

Granny stitch is worked using groups of three treble crochet stitches all worked into the same space. It can be worked in lots of different shapes, but in this book we will be working it in straight rows, or in joined rows called rounds. Granny stitch is worked into the spaces between groups, rather than into the stitches, which makes it quick to crochet, and produces a slightly thicker fabric than regular stitches, which is why we'll only be using double knitting (DK) or 4 ply (fingering) weight yarn for these projects.

Tools & Materials

There are a few things that you will need to get going on these projects. Investing in the right tools makes life easier and pretty ones make it all the more enjoyable!

Tools

HOOKS

To make the patterns in this book, you'll need a set of crochet hooks ranging from 3mm to 5mm (US D/3 to H/8). When making garments, it's very important to work to the correct tension (gauge), so that your garments fit correctly. Therefore, it's always good to have a range of crochet hooks in all sizes, so that you can adjust your hook to match the tension given in the pattern. Making garments means lots of repetitive rows, so it's important to have hooks that are comfortable to use and well made. Hooks with rubber handles are great, as they have more flexibility and allow for a good grip.

STITCH MARKERS

You will also need a set of stitch markers for marking certain points in your work, especially when working top-down garments. Locking stitch markers are the best choice as they can be closed and won't fall off. Choose plastic ones over wire, as their points are more rounded and won't catch in your work. Look for stitch markers with more flexibility rather than cheap brittle ones that snap easily.

TAPE MEASURE

To make the garments in this book fit, it's important that you measure your bust circumference (with your bra on), so that you can choose the correct size to follow. You should also check the width of your garment as you work, against the width given in the size table. Sometimes our tension can change over a project, so keeping an eye on the width and length is a good way to know if you're on track. You'll need a good tape measure for this. A retractable one is useful for carrying around when you're crocheting on the go, as it won't get tangled in your hooks!

RULER

You'll also need a small ruler to check your tension. A ruler is better than a tape measure for this as it is easier to hold it down and you can keep it flat with one hand. A clear ruler makes counting your stitches easier.

PINS

Some long pins are needed for pinning your work together and you'll need rust-free blocking pins for blocking your pieces to size.

SCISSORS AND YARN NEEDLES

Finally, a small pair of scissors and some metal yarn needles are essential, for cutting your yarn and weaving in your ends.

CROCHET HOOK SIZES

Use this table to convert metric hook sizes to their US equivalents.

Millimetres (UK)	US Size Range
2mm	–
2.25mm	B/1
2.50mm	
2.75mm	C/2
3mm	–
3.125mm	D
3.25mm	D/3
3.50mm	E/4
3.75mm	F/5
4mm	G/6
4.25mm	G
4.50mm	7
5mm	H/8
5.25mm	I
5.50mm	I/9
5.75mm	J
6mm	J/10

Materials

YARN

Crochet creates a much thicker fabric than knitting, so all the patterns in this book use 4 ply (fingering) or DK weight yarn. Cotton or cotton-blend yarns are best for summer tops, as they keep you cool, while acrylic and wool are best for winter garments. Acrylic is machine washable and can be tumble dried (making it great for children's clothes) and there are some great premium acrylic yarns, which have a lovely matte texture. Wool is beautiful and much warmer, and although most is hand wash only, it transports moisture away from the body, causing less bacteria build up, and therefore less odour than other fibres, which means the need for washing is minimal.

TIP

TO HAND WASH YOUR WOOL GARMENTS, POUR A LITTLE WOOL WASH LIQUID INTO SOME WARM WATER AND ALLOW YOUR GARMENT TO SOAK FOR A WHILE. THEN RINSE AND SQUEEZE OUT ANY EXCESS WATER. ROLL THE GARMENT UP IN A TOWEL AND CONTINUE TO SQUEEZE OUT THE WATER, TAKING CARE NOT TO STRETCH IT. FINALLY, LAY YOUR GARMENT OUT FLAT ON AN AIRER TO DRY. DO NOT HANG IT UP AS THE WEIGHT OF THE WATER WILL STRETCH IT.

Use this table to work out which yarn weight category each yarn type falls into.

Yarn weight category	Super fine	Fine	Light	Medium	Bulky	Super bulky
Types of yarn in category	4 ply, Sock, Fingering, Baby	Sport, Baby	DK, Light Worsted	Aran, Worsted, Afghan	Chunky, Craft, Rug	Bulky, Super Chunky, Roving

SUBSTITUTING YARN

If you substitute any of the yarns in this book, ensure you look for a yarn with similar metres per gram (yards per ounce) to the yarn given in the pattern. Divide the number of metres (yards) by the number of grams (ounces) in a ball to work this out. This will ensure that you don't end up with a yarn that's too thin or too thick for the pattern. For example, the V-neck Jumper uses a very thin lightweight wool and alpaca blend, and you will not get the same drape and slouch using a thicker, stiffer yarn. Top-down garments also tend to stretch more, as they don't have the stability of seams to support them, so if you substitute a heavier yarn, you may find your garment stretches due to the overall weight. It's worth noting that even yarns within the same yarn weight category can vary greatly in thickness. For example, the yarn used for the Striped Cardigan is a thick DK cotton blend, with a tension of four-and-a-half granny stitches to 10cm (4in), which wouldn't be achievable with the yarn used in the Patchwork Jumper, which is a much thinner DK. Therefore, as exciting as starting a garment is, it's important to take time to research your yarn choice before jumping in.

Granny Stitch Techniques

Getting Started

Before you dive in, take some time to read through the guidance on this page as it will help you to understand how the patterns work.

TERMINOLOGY

The patterns in this book use UK terminology. However, if you are used to working with US terminology, please refer to the conversion table below.

UK term	US term
double crochet	single crochet
half treble crochet	half double crochet
treble crochet	double crochet
foundation double crochet	foundation single crochet

ABBREVIATIONS

The following abbreviations have been used for the patterns in this book:

blo = back loop only

ch(s) = chain(s)

dc = double crochet

dc2tog = double crochet 2 together (decrease)

fdc = foundation double crochet

flo = front loop only

htr = half treble crochet

prev = previous

rep = repeat

rs = right side

st(s) = stitch(es)

sl st = slip stitch

tr = treble crochet

tr2tog = treble crochet 2 together (decrease)

ws = wrong side

yo = yarn over

FOLLOWING THE PATTERNS

Below you'll find some useful guidelines to following the patterns in this book.

- 3ch counts as the first treble. (1dc, 2ch works as a great alternative to 3ch). 2ch counts as the first half treble. 1ch does not count as the first double crochet.

- Instructions for each garment size are written in brackets in the following order: XS (S, M, L, XL, 2XL, 3XL, 4XL). When no instructions are needed for a particular size, an x will appear in its place. For example: 2 (x, 3, x, 4, x, 4, x) sps.

- Left and right side: If the pattern asks you to work up the left side, it is referring to the left side of the garment if you were wearing it.

- Right and wrong side: Hold your fabric so that the right side of the stitches on row 1 are facing you. This is the right side. When the wrong side of the same stitches face you you, this is the wrong side of the garment.

- Substituting yarn: If you are going to substitute the yarn used in the book for a different yarn, always choose a yarn with very similar metres per gram (yards per ounce). This information can be found on the yarn ball band.

Granny Stitch Basics

Granny stitch is a little different to regular crochet stitches, as the rows are offset. Take some time to perfect your technique before starting out on a project and you'll be making beautiful garments in no time.

WORKING THE GRANNY STITCH

To start off working in granny stitch you'll need to create a chain, and then work groups of trebles across your chain. For row 1 you will work a treble stitch at either end. We use the last 3 chains from our starting chain to count as the first treble stitch at the start. At the end of your row, you will turn the work over, so the wrong side of the stitches are facing you. Then you will work back in the same direction you came from. Because the stitches are offset, on row 2 you will work two treble stitches at either end but have one less group across the row. Row 3 then follows the same pattern as row 1 and they continue to alternate.

READING SYMBOL CHARTS

Some patterns are accompanied by stitch symbol diagrams to help you put your stitches in the correct places. Each stitch is represented by a symbol, which you will find in the key below. Whenever you see the symbol for a treble crochet, work a treble crochet stitch into the space shown on the chart, and so on. Because we are working in granny stitch throughout this book, the treble stitches are often worked into spaces rather than into stitches.

STITCH KEY

- ◦ ch(s) = chain(s)
- + dc = double crochet
- T htr = half treble crochet
- ⋎ granny cluster/group
- · sl st = slip stitch
- ◗ stitch marker
- ⊤ tr = treble crochet

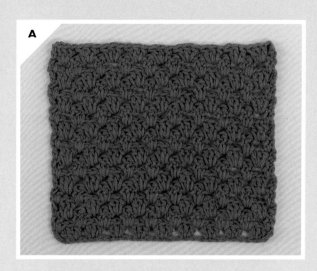

A

TENSION (GAUGE)

When making anything wearable, it is important to ensure your tension matches that given in the pattern, otherwise the garment or accessory will not fit as it should. In this book, tension is measured over 10cm (4in). If you have fewer stitches or rows to 10cm (4in) than the pattern tension states, your piece will end up bigger than the measurements given, so you need to use a smaller hook. Try going down half a hook size to start with. If you have more stitches or rows to 10cm (4in) than the tension states, then your piece will end up smaller and you need to use a bigger hook. If you substitute a different yarn and your fabric looks too dense or too holey with the correct tension, you may need to look at choosing a thicker or thinner yarn for your project.

MAKING A TENSION SWATCH

This can be tricky if you don't know how to get started. The pattern below is for a square that is 9 granny groups wide and 15 rows high, which should be ample for you to check your tension against the pattern (A). You can also follow the pattern on the symbol chart.

Starting chain: 31ch.

R1: 3tr in fifth ch from the hook, (miss 2 chs, 3tr in next ch) 8 times, miss 1 ch, 1tr in last ch, turn.

R2: 3ch, 1tr in same sp, 3tr in each each of next 8 sps, 1tr in last sp, 1tr in top of 3ch, turn.

R3: 3ch, (3tr in next sp) 9 times, 1tr in top of 3ch, turn.

Alternate between R2 and R3 until you have 15 rows. Fasten off.

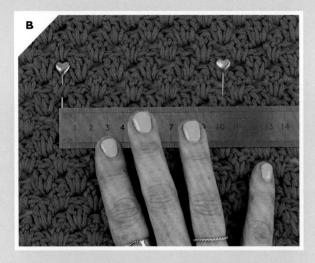

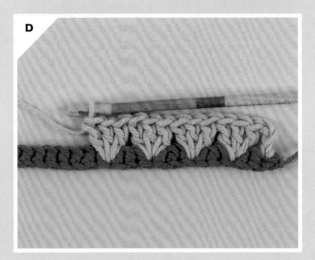

To measure the stitches, place your ruler in the centre of the space before the first group, and then count how many groups fall into the measurement given. For example, if the tension given is '5 groups to 10cm (4in)', you want the 10cm (4in) mark to fall halfway across the space after the fifth group. If the tension is '4.5 groups to 10cm (4in)', then you want your 10cm (4in) mark to fall halfway across the fifth group (B).

To measure the rows on your swatch, place your ruler at the top of a group in the middle of your swatch and count how many rows fall within the given measurement (C).

SET UP ROWS OR ROUNDS

When starting off in granny stitch, the patterns in this book require you to work a set up row, to give your first row of granny stitch a firmer foundation. This can be done either by working a foundation double crochet row or round (fdc), or by making a chain followed by a row of double crochet. The foundation double crochet creates a stretchier base, so this is the suggested method. For full instructions on working foundation double crochet see Crochet Techniques.

Keeping the right side of the fdc foundation row facing you, work the first row of granny stitch over the double crochet stitches and into the chains at the bottom. This ensures that the first row of granny stitch does not have big gaps around them (D).

Taking It Further

This page contains some useful guidance on shaping your work, adding rib and changing colour. Practise these techniques on your tension swatch first and then refer back to this guidance later on.

ADAPTING GARMENT LENGTHS

Granny stitches are offset, this means that they work in a repeating pattern of two rows. Because of this, if you are lengthening or shortening a garment you should always add or remove rows (or rounds) in pairs to keep in sync with the pattern.

NECK AND ARMHOLE SHAPING

To create a diagonal or a curve in granny stitch you will work a series of staggered rows that end in groups of two trebles (A).

SLIP STITCHING AND ADDING RIB

The patterns in this book use double crochet (US single crochet) ribbing. This is done by working a starting chain, working double crochets along the chain, and then anchoring the end of the row to the garment with several slip stitches before working back in the same direction. This works well along the top or bottom of a straight row. However, if you are working down row edges or around curved edges, like necklines or armholes, you will need to slip stitch around the armhole or neckline first using the same colour as the ribbing (B). (It may be easier to go up half a hook size for this part, to ensure your slip stitches aren't too small to work into). You can then work the ribbing as usual, in your normal hook size, anchoring it to the back loop of the slip stitches at the end of every other row (C). This will give a neat and consistent look to your ribbing.

CHANGING COLOUR

To change yarn colour either at the end of a row or mid row: On the last stitch of the last group, work the last yo in the new colour and drop the previous colour to the wrong side of the work. Work the next instruction in the new colour (D).

If you are going to be using the previous colour again later in the row you will need to carry it across your work. Once you have dropped the colour, lay it towards the top of the row below, on the wrong side of your work and crochet over it with each group. Image E shows the back of the current row.

When you work back across the next row, any contrast-coloured yarn that you have carried across may be visible in the spaces between groups. If this is the case, pick up and crochet under the carried yarn as you work into the spaces, to hide it (E).

When you need to pick it up again it can sometimes be visible as you bring it up the side of your last stitch to yarn over. To avoid this, do not carry it under the last stitch, drop it to the back of your work, then work the last stitch. When you come to do the last yarn over of the last stitch, the yarn will be coming in at an angle and will be less visible. Image F shows the back of the current row.

If you are working in stripes, it is possible to float your yarn up the sides of your work to avoid cutting it at the end of each row and having lots of ends to weave in. To make this work you will need to have an odd number of colours in the garment, perhaps three or five (unless you are working in the round or working two-row stripes, then you can have any number).

At the end of the row, work the last yarn over of the last stitch in the new colour and let the previous colour hang down the side. Work the next row in the new colour. When you reach the end of the row, change to the next colour by bringing it up the side (being careful not to pull too tight) and using it to work the last yarn over. Let the previous colour drop to the side (G).

Just remember that every time you turn your work you will need to bring your attached balls with you to avoid a tangle!

A

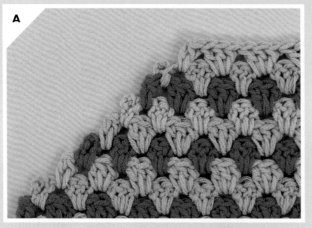

B

C

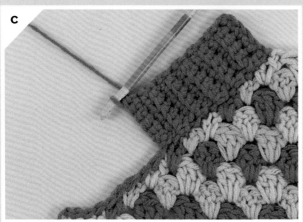

D

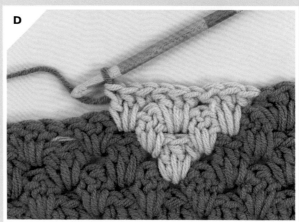

E

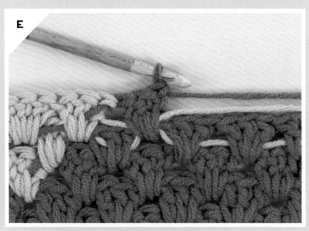

F

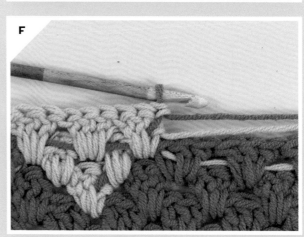

G

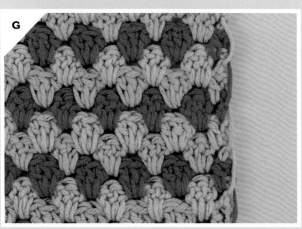

TIP

YOU CAN ALSO FLOAT YARNS WHEN WORKING IN THE ROUND. AT THE END OF YOUR ROUND, JOIN WITH A SLIP STITCH, BUT PULL UP A LARGE LOOP, PASS THE YARN BALL THROUGH IT AND PULL TIGHT TO SECURE THE YARN.

Projects

Folk Blouse

This cute blouse is perfect for mild spring days and features a colourful granny stripe bib, and a ruffled sleeve cap, which will brighten up any outfit.

✧ YOU WILL NEED

Hook: 4mm (G/6)

Scissors

Yarn needle

Yarn: King Cole Bamboo Cotton DK. 50% Cotton, 50% Bamboo, 100g (3½oz) = 230m (252yd), in the following shades:

- Yarn A: White 530
- Yarn B: Fuchsia 536
- Yarn C: Crimson 634

✧ PATTERN NOTES

Yarn weight: DK

Tension: 5 x 3tr groups and 10 rows = 10cm (4in)

Folk Blouse Schematic

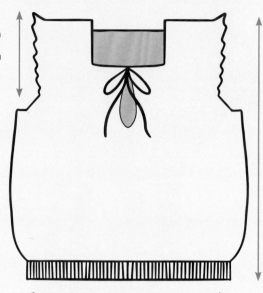

15 (16, 17, 18, 19, 20, 21, 22)cm

6 (6¼, 6¾, 7, 7½, 8, 8¼, 8¾)in

49.5 (51.5, 53.5, 55.5, 57.5, 59.5, 61.5, 63.5)cm

19½ (20¼, 21, 21⅞, 22½, 23⅝, 24⅝, 25)in

40 (44, 50, 54, 60, 64, 70, 74)cm

15¾ (17⅜, 19¾, 21¼, 23⅝, 25¼, 27½, 29⅛)in

Yardage and Sizing

YARN QUANTITIES:

	XS	S	M	L	XL	2XL	3XL	4XL
Yarn A	374g (13¼oz)/ 860m (940½yd)	389g (13¾oz)/ 895m (978¾yd)	414g (14⅝oz)/ 952m (1041¼yd)	435g (15⅜oz)/ 1000m (1093⅝yd)	458g (16¼oz)/ 1053m (1151⅜yd)	476g (16¾oz)/ 1095m (1197½yd)	505g (17¾oz)/ 1162m (1270¾yd)	518g (18¼oz)/ 1191m (1302½yd)
Yarn B	18g (⅝oz)/ 41m (45yd)	18g (⅝oz)/ 41m (45yd)	19g (⅝oz) /44m (48⅛yd)	19g (⅝oz)/ 44m (48⅛yd)	27g (1oz)/ 62m (67¾yd)	27g (1oz)/ 62m (67¾yd)	28g (1oz)/ 64m (70yd)	28g (1oz)/ 64m (70yd)
Yarn C	11g (⅜oz)/ 25m (27⅜yd)	11g (⅜oz)/ 25m (27⅜yd)	11g (⅜oz)/ 25m (27⅜yd)	11g (⅜oz)/ 25m (27⅜yd)	19g (⅝oz)/ 44m (48⅛yd)	19g (⅝oz)/ 44m (48⅛yd)	19g (⅝oz)/ 44m (48⅛yd)	19g (⅝oz) /44m (48⅛yd)

SIZING CHART: 3–5CM (1¼–2IN) POSITIVE EASE DEPENDING ON SIZE

	XS	S	M	L	XL	2XL	3XL	4XL
Bust	75cm (29½in)	85cm (33½in)	95cm (37⅜in)	105cm (41⅜in)	115cm (45¼in)	125cm (49¼in)	135cm (53⅛in)	145cm (57⅛in)
Garment circumference	80cm (31½in)	88cm (34⅝in)	100cm (39⅜in)	108cm (42½in)	120cm (47¼in)	128cm (50⅜in)	140cm (55⅛in)	148cm (58¼in)
Garment width	40cm (15¾in)	44cm (17⅜in)	50cm (19¾in)	54cm (21¼in)	60cm (23⅝in)	64cm (25¼in)	70cm (27½in)	74cm (29⅛in)
Garment length	49.5cm (19½in)	51.5cm (20¼in)	53.5cm (21in)	55.5cm (21⅞in)	57.5cm (22⅝in)	59.5cm (23⅜in)	61.5cm (24¼in)	63.5cm (25in)

Construction

Work back and forth from the centre in a U shape to form the front and back. The side and shoulder seams are then sewn up and a ruffle is added around the upper armhole.

Front

BIB (A)

Set up row: Using yarn A, 43 fdc.

Alternatively, 44ch. 1dc in second ch from hook, 1dc in each ch to end, turn.

On the next row you are going to work groups of 3tr over the dc sts and into the bottom ch.

R1 (rs): Attach yarn B to top of last st, 3ch, miss 1 ch, (3tr in next ch, miss 2 chs) 6 times, 3tr in next ch, 3ch, 3tr in next ch, 3ch, (3tr in next ch, miss 2 chs) 6 times, 3tr in next ch, miss 1 ch, 1tr in last ch, turn. Fasten off yarn B. 15 3tr groups.

R2: Attach yarn C to top of last tr, 3ch, 1tr in same sp, 3tr in each of next 6 sps, (3tr, 3ch, 3tr in 3ch sp) twice, 3tr in next 6 sps, 1tr in last sp, 1tr in top of 3ch, turn. Fasten off yarn C. 16 3tr groups.

R3: Attach yarn A to top of last tr, 3ch, 3tr in each of next 7 sps, (3tr, 3ch, 3tr) in 3ch sp, 3tr in next sp, (3tr, 3ch, 3tr) in 3ch sp, 3tr in each of next 7 sps, 1tr in top of 3ch, turn. Fasten off yarn A. 19 3tr groups.

R4: Attach yarn B to top of last tr, 3ch, 1tr in same sp, 3tr in each of next 7 sps, (3tr, 3ch, 3tr) in 3ch sp, 3tr in next 2 sps, (3tr, 3ch, 3tr) in 3ch sp, 3tr in next 7 sps, 1tr in last sp, 1tr in top of 3ch, turn. Fasten off yarn B. 20 3tr groups.

R5: Attach yarn C to top of last tr, 3ch, 3tr in each of next 8 sps, (3tr, 3ch, 3tr) in 3ch sp, 3tr in next 3 sps, (3tr, 3ch, 3tr) in 3ch sp, 3tr in each of next 8 sps, 1tr in top of 3ch, turn. Fasten off yarn C. 23 3tr groups.

R6: Attach yarn A to top of last tr, 3ch, 1tr in same sp, 3tr in each of next 8 sps, (3tr, 3ch, 3tr) in 3ch sp, 3tr in next 4 sps, (3tr, 3ch, 3tr) in 3ch sp, 3tr in next 8 sps, 1tr in last sp, 1tr in top of 3ch, turn. 24 3tr groups.

Sizes XL–4XL only: Work R7 in yarn B and R8 in yarn C.

R7: 3ch, 3tr in each sp to first 3ch sp, (3tr, 3ch, 3tr) in 3ch sp, 3tr in each sp to second 3ch sp, (3tr, 3ch, 3tr) in 3ch sp, 3tr in each sp to end, 1tr in top of 3ch, turn. 27 3tr groups.

R8: 3ch, 1tr in same sp, 3tr in each sp to first 3ch sp, (3tr, 3ch, 3tr) in sp, 3tr in each sp to second 3ch sp, (3tr, 3ch, 3tr) in sp, 3tr in each sp to end, 1tr in last sp, 1tr in top of 3ch, turn. 28 3tr groups.

Sizes XS (S, M, L) only: At end of R8, 18 (18, 21, 21) ch, turn. Do not fasten off.

Sizes XL (2XL, 3XL, 4XL) only: Rep R7 and R8 in yarn A. 32 3tr groups. At end of R10, 24 (24, 27, 27) ch, turn. Do not fasten off.

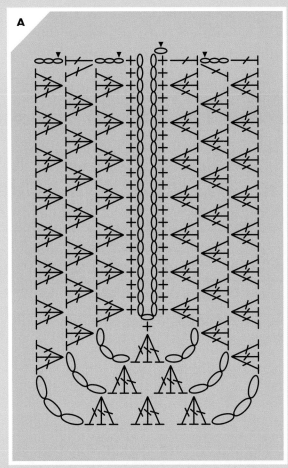

CHART SHOWS FRONT BIB SECTION

SHOULDER EXTENSION ROW

Using a separate ball of yarn A, attach yarn to top of 3ch at start of last row, 16 (16, 19, 19, 22, 22, 25, 25) ch, fasten off.

Using working yarn from end of last row, 3tr in fifth ch from hook, [miss 2 chs, 3tr in next ch] 4 (4, 5, 5, 6, 6, 7, 7) times, miss last ch, 3tr in sp after 2tr and in each sp to first 3ch sp, (3tr, 3ch, 3tr) in 3ch sp, 3tr in each sp to second 3ch sp, (3tr, 3ch, 3tr) in 3ch sp, 3tr in each sp to last 2tr, miss 1ch, 3tr in next ch, [miss 2chs, 3tr in next ch] 4 (4, 5, 5, 6, 6, 7, 7) times, miss 1 ch, 1tr in last ch, turn. You will have 16 (16, 17, 17, 19, 19, 20, 20) 3tr groups down each side and 9 (9, 9, 9, 11, 11, 11, 11) 3tr groups across the base.

MAIN SHOULDER ROW 1

3ch, 1tr in same sp, 3tr in each sp to first 3ch sp, (3tr, 3ch, 3tr) in 3ch sp, 3tr in each sp to second 3ch sp, (3tr, 3ch, 3tr) in 3ch sp, 3tr in each sp to end, 1tr in last sp, 1tr in top of 3ch, turn. 42 (42, 44, 44, 50, 50, 52, 52) 3tr groups.

MAIN SHOULDER ROW 2

3ch, 3tr in each sp to first 3ch sp, (3tr, 3ch, 3tr) in 3ch sp, 3tr in each sp to second 3ch sp, (3tr, 3ch, 3tr) in 3ch sp, 3tr in each sp to end, 1tr in top of 3ch, turn. 45 (45, 47, 47, 53, 53, 55, 55) 3tr groups.

Main shoulder R1 and R2 form pattern. Rep pattern until you have 18 (18, 19, 20, 20, 21, 22, 22) rows from start, ending in 58 (58, 63, 64, 66, 69, 72, 72) 3tr groups. Fasten off, turn.

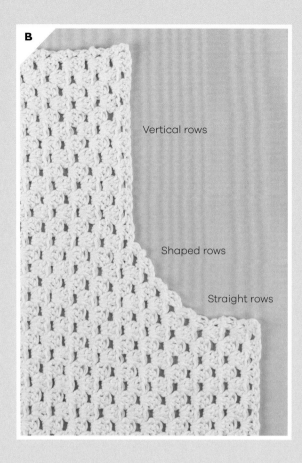

Vertical rows

Shaped rows

Straight rows

SHAPE ARMHOLES (B)

R1: With ws of sts in previous row facing you, count 8 (8, 8, 8, 7, 8, 8, 8) sps from end of last row and attach yarn in sp. 3ch, 1tr in sp, 3tr in next 12 (12, 14, 14, 16, 16, 17, 17) sps, (3tr, 3ch, 3tr) in 3ch sp, 3tr in each sp across the base, (3tr, 3ch, 3tr) in 3ch sp, 3tr in next 12 (12, 14, 14, 16, 16, 17, 17) sps, 2tr in next sp, turn.

Size XS only: Work from Straighten Armholes section.

Sizes S–4XL only – R2: Sl st across top of next st, sl st into next sp, 3ch, 1tr in sp, 3tr in next x (12, 14, 14, 16, 16, 17, 17) sps, (3tr, 3ch, 3tr) in 3ch sp, 3tr in each sp across the base, (3tr, 3ch, 3tr) in 3ch sp, 3tr in next x (12, 14, 14, 16, 16, 17, 17) sps, 2tr in next sp, turn.

Rep R2 x (0, 2, 2, 5, 5, 5, 6) more times until you have x (2, 4, 4, 7, 7, 7, 8) shaped rows. You will have 13 (13, 15, 15, 17, 17, 18, 18) 3tr groups along each edge and 19 (20, 23, 24, 27, 28, 29, 30) 3tr groups along the base, turn.

Sizes 3XL and 4XL only: Work from Side Extension 1 section.

STRAIGHTEN ARMHOLES SIZES XS TO 2XL ONLY

R1: 3ch, 3tr in next 13 (13, 15, 15, 17, 17, x, x) sps, (3tr, 3ch, 3tr) in 3ch sp, 3tr in each sp across the base, (3tr, 3ch, 3tr) in 3ch sp, 3tr in next 13 (13, 15, 15, 17, 17, x, x) sps, 1tr in top of 3ch, turn.

Size XS only: Fasten off and work from Length Extension section. You will have 14 groups down each side and 20 groups across the base.

Sizes XL (2XL) only: Work from Side Extension 1 section. You will have 18 (18) groups down each side and 28 (29) groups across the base.

R2: 3ch, 1tr in same sp, 3tr in next x (13, 15, 15, x, x, x, x) sps, (3tr, 3ch, 3tr) in 3ch sp, 3tr in each sp across the base, (3tr, 3ch, 3tr) in 3ch sp, 3tr in next x (13, 15, 15, x, x, x, x) sps, 1tr in last sp, 1tr in top of 3ch, turn.

Sizes S (M) only: Fasten off. You will have (14) 16 groups down each side and 22 (25) groups across the base.

Size S only: Work from Length Extension section.

Size L only – R3: 3ch, 3tr in next 16 sps, (3tr, 3ch, 3tr) in 3ch sp, 3tr in each sp across the base, (3tr, 3ch, 3tr) in 3ch sp, 3tr in next 16 sps, 1tr in top of 3ch, fasten off. You will have 17 groups down each side and 27 groups across the base.

LENGTH EXTENSION

Sizes XS (S) only:

With rs facing out, attach yarn to 3ch sp in bottom right corner.

R1: 3ch, 1tr in 3ch sp, 3tr in each sp to end, 2tr in 3ch sp at end, turn. 19 (21) 3tr groups.

R2: 3ch, 3tr in each sp to end, 1tr in top of 3ch, turn. 20 (22) 3tr groups.

R3: 3ch, 1tr in same sp, 3tr in each sp to end, 1tr in last sp, 1tr in top of 3ch, turn.

R4: Rep R2. Fasten off.

SIDE EXTENSION 1

Sizes XL (2XL, 3XL, 4XL) only: You have reached the given length and will now add extra rows on either side to increase width. Sizes XL and 4XL this will be your right side, 2XL and 3XL this will be your left side.

R1: 3ch, (sizes XL and 2XL only - 1tr in same sp), 3tr in next 17 (17, 18, 18) sps, 2tr in 3ch sp, turn.

R2: 3ch, 3tr in next 18 sps, (sizes 3XL and 4XL only - 1tr in last sp), 1tr in top of 3ch, turn.

Size XL: Fasten off.

R3: 3ch, (size 2XL only - 1tr in same sp), 3tr in next x (17, 18, 18) sps, 1tr in last sp, 1tr in top of 3ch, turn.

Size 2XL: Fasten off.

Rep R3 x (x, 3, 4) more times. Fasten off.

SIDE EXTENSION 2

Sizes XL (2XL, 3XL, 4XL) only: Sizes XL and 4XL this will be your left side, 2XL and 3XL this will be your right side. Attach yarn to 3ch sp at bottom corner.

R1: 3ch, 1tr in same sp, 3tr in next 17 (17, 18, 18) sps, (sizes XL and 2XL only - 1tr in last sp), 1tr in top of 3ch, turn.

R2: 3ch, (sizes 3XL and 4XL only - 1tr in same sp), 3tr in next 18 sps, 1tr in top of 3ch, turn.

Size XL: Fasten off.

R3: 3ch, 1tr in same sp, 3tr in next x (17, 18, 18) sps, (size 2XL only - 1tr in last sp), 1tr in top of 3ch.

Size 2XL: Fasten off.

Rep R3 x (x, 3, 4) more times. Fasten off.

Back

Set up row: 31 (31, 34, 34, 37, 37, 40, 40) ch. 1dc in second ch from hook, 1dc in each ch to end, 2 more dc in last ch, 1dc in other side of next ch and in other side of each ch up opposite side, turn (C).

On the next row you are going to work groups of 3tr over the dc sts and into the bottom ch.

R1 (rs): 3ch, miss 1 ch, (3tr in next ch, miss 2 chs) 9 (9, 10, 10, 11, 11, 12, 12) times, 3tr, 3ch, 3tr, 3ch, 3tr in same ch at end, (miss 2 chs, 3tr in next ch) 9 (9, 10, 10, 11, 11, 12, 12) times, miss 1 ch, 1tr in last ch, turn. 21 (21, 23, 23, 25, 25, 27, 27) 3tr groups.

R2: 3ch, 1tr in same sp, 3tr in each of next 9 (9, 10, 10, 11, 11, 12, 12) sps, (3tr, 3ch, 3tr in 3ch sp) twice, 3tr in each of next 9 (9, 10, 10, 11, 11, 12, 12) sps, 1tr in last sp, 1tr in top of 3ch, turn. 22 (22, 24, 24, 26, 26, 28, 28) 3tr groups.

R3: 3ch, 3tr in each sp to 3ch sp (3tr, 3ch, 3tr) in 3ch sp, 3tr in each sp to next 3ch sp, (3tr, 3ch, 3tr) in 3ch sp, 3tr in each sp to end, 1tr in top of 3ch, turn.

R4: 3ch, 1tr in same sp, 3tr in each sp to 3ch sp (3tr, 3ch, 3tr) in 3ch sp, 3tr in each sp to next 3ch sp, (3tr, 3ch, 3tr) in 3ch sp, 3tr in each sp to last sp, 1tr in last sp, 1tr in top of 3ch, turn.

R3 and R4 form pattern. Rep pattern until you have 8 (8, 8, 8, 10, 10, 10, 10) rows. At end of last row 9ch, turn.

SHOULDER EXTENSION ROW

Using a separate ball of yarn A, attach yarn to top of 3ch at start of last row and 7ch, fasten off.

Using working yarn from end of last row, 3tr in fifth ch from hook, miss 2 chs, 3tr in next ch, 3tr in sp after 2tr and in each sp to first 3ch sp, (3tr, 3ch, 3tr) in 3ch sp, 3tr in each sp to second 3ch sp, (3tr, 3ch, 3tr) in 3ch sp, 3tr in each sp to last 2tr, miss 1ch, 3tr in next ch, miss 2chs, 3tr in next ch, miss 1 ch, 1tr in last ch, turn. You will have 16 (16, 17, 17, 19, 19, 20, 20) 3tr groups down each side and 9 (9, 9, 9, 11, 11, 11, 11) 3tr groups across the base.

Work from Main Shoulder Row 1 on front to end of front, including side/length extensions.

Block your panels to given dimensions. With rs facing each other, sew up shoulder seams and sew up or sl st seams.

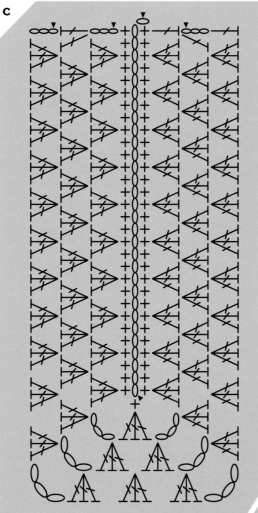

C

RIBBED HEM BAND

Start with the rs of body facing you. If you finished the body on a ws row you will need to turn. Attach yarn to bottom of right-side seam.

Set up round sizes XS–L only: 1ch, 1dc in top of each st to end, join to top of first dc with a sl st. Do not turn.

Set up round sizes XL–4XL only: 1ch, *dc evenly across the rows on your side extensions until you reach the 3tr groups section (work 5 sts per 2 rows), 1dc in top of each st across 3tr group section**, rep from * to **, dc evenly across the rows on your side extensions to end, join to top of first dc with a sl st, do not turn.

R1: 10ch, 1dc in second ch from hook, (1ch missed does not count as stitch), 1dc in each of next 8 chs, sl st blo across next 3 sts to anchor your rib to the body, turn. 9 sts.

R2: 1dc blo in next 9 sts, turn.

R3: 1ch, 1dc blo in next 9sts, sl st blo across next 3 sts on body, turn.

R2 and R3 form pattern. Rep pattern to end and seam edges together on ws using slip stitch.

NECK TRIM AND TIE

Work with rs facing out.

R1: Using yarn A, 70ch, sl st in second ch from hook and in each ch to end. With rs of top facing out, sl st to right front corner of bib, under last fdc st, dc evenly across row edges to first corner (approx 5 dc per 2 sts), dc2tog at corner, 1dc in each ch along shoulder extension past shoulder seam and down to second corner, dc2tog at second corner, dc evenly across row edges at back neck to third corner, dc2tog at third corner, 1dc in each ch along shoulder extension, past shoulder seam, to fourth corner, dc2tog at fourth corner, dc evenly across row edges to left front corner, 70ch, sl st in second ch from hook and in each ch to end, 1sl st in each fdc st in U-shaped set up row back to right front corner.

R2: 1ch, 1dc in each st around neckline (miss out the ties) to left front corner, working a dc2tog across each of the four corners as before, fasten off.

SLEEVE TRIM AND RUFFLES

Work with rs facing out.

R1: Join yarn A to top of side seam, at base of armhole. 1ch, dc evenly along straight and shaped side rows to vertical rows (work 5 sts per 2 rows). Sl st into first tr of first 3tr group, 3ch, 2tr in same st, miss second tr of group, 3ch, 3tr in third tr of group, 3ch, *3tr in first tr of next group, miss second tr of group, 3ch, 3tr in third tr of group, 3ch** to shoulder seam, 3tr, 3ch at shoulder seam, rep from *to ** from next 3tr group to end of vertical section, sl st to top of first shaped row, dc evenly along shaped and straight side rows to end, join to top of first dc with a sl st, fasten off.

Tip: If your underarms gape, work 3 sts per 2 rows across the straight and shaped rows only.

R2 optional sleeve trim: Attach yarn B to top of first st in ruffle section. 1ch, (1dc in each st of 3tr group, 3dc in 3ch sp) to last 3tr group of ruffle section, 1dc in each st of group, fasten off.

Rep on opposite armhole. Weave in ends.

Tank Top

This colourful tank top will get you ready for the warmer days ahead. Wear it over a white tee or a billowy blouse and stand out from the crowd. Worked in a soft Merino blend, it will keep your core nice and snug.

◇ YOU WILL NEED

Hooks: 4.5mm (7), 4mm (G/6) for the ribbing

Scissors

Yarn needle

Yarn: Scheepjes Merino Soft. 50% Superwash Merino wool, 25% Microfibre, 25% Acrylic, 50g (1¾oz) = 105m (115yd), in the following shades:

- Yarn A: Dali 608
- Yarn B: Matisse 635
- Yarn C: Titian 647
- Yarn D: Degas 632
- Yarn E: Van Gogh 641

◇ PATTERN NOTES

Yarn weight: DK

Tension: 4.5 x 3tr groups and 10.5 rows = 10cm (4in)

Tank Top Schematic

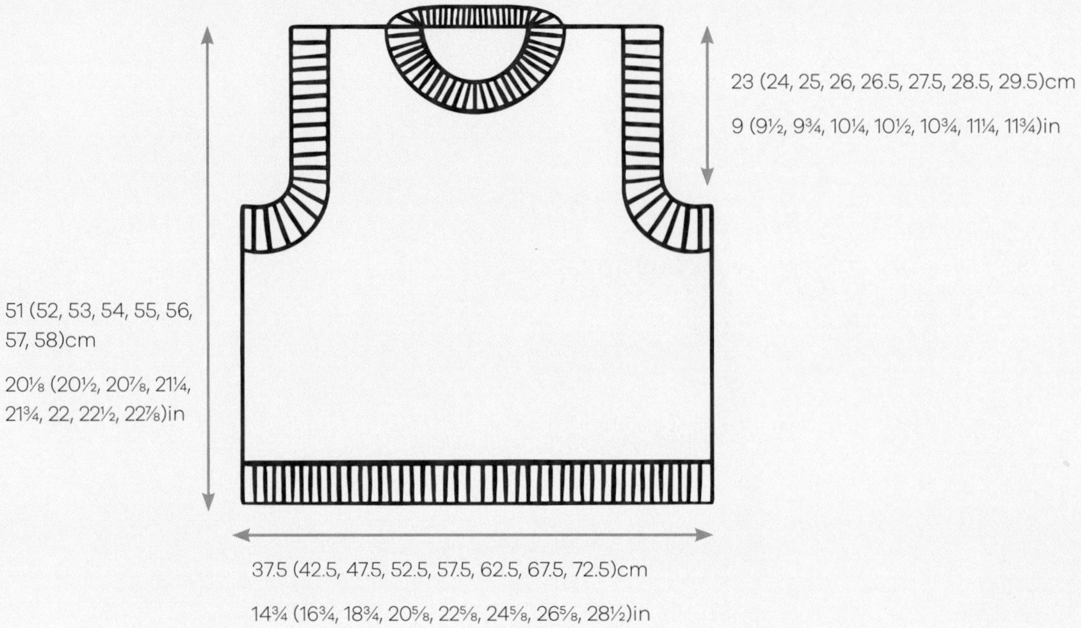

23 (24, 25, 26, 26.5, 27.5, 28.5, 29.5)cm

9 (9½, 9¾, 10¼, 10½, 10¾, 11¼, 11¾)in

51 (52, 53, 54, 55, 56, 57, 58)cm

20⅛ (20½, 20⅞, 21¼, 21¾, 22, 22½, 22⅞)in

37.5 (42.5, 47.5, 52.5, 57.5, 62.5, 67.5, 72.5)cm

14¾ (16¾, 18¾, 20⅝, 22⅝, 24⅝, 26⅝, 28½)in

Yardage and Sizing

YARN QUANTITIES:

	XS	S	M	L	XL	2XL	3XL	4XL
Yarn A	120g (4¼oz)/ 252m (275½yd)	125g (4½oz)/ 263m (287½yd)	130g (4⅝oz)/ 273m (298½yd)	136g (4¾oz)/ 286m (312¾yd)	141g (5oz)/ 296m (323¾yd)	146g (5⅛oz)/ 307m (335¾yd)	151g (5¼oz)/ 317m (346¾yd)	156g (5½oz)/ 328m (358¾yd)
Yarn B	49g (1¾oz)/ 103m (112½yd)	55g (2oz)/ 116m (126¾yd)	61g (2⅛oz)/ 128m (140yd)	69g (2½oz)/ 145m (158½yd)	75g (2⅝oz)/ 158m (172¾yd)	81g (2⅞oz)/ 170m (186yd)	90g (3¼oz)/ 189m (206½yd)	95g (3⅜oz)/ 200m (218¾yd)
Yarn C	49g (1¾oz)/ 103m (112½yd)	55g (2oz)/ 116m (126¾yd)	61g (2⅛oz)/ 128m (140yd)	69g (2½oz)/ 145m (158½yd)	75g (2⅝oz)/ 158m (172¾yd)	81g (2⅞oz)/ 170m (186yd)	90g (3¼oz)/ 189m (206½yd)	95g (3⅜oz)/ 200m (218¾yd)
Yarn D	49g (1¾oz)/ 103m (112½yd)	55g (2oz)/ 116m (126¾yd)	61g (2⅛oz)/ 128m (140yd)	69g (2½oz)/ 145m (158½yd)	75g (2⅝oz)/ 158m (172¾yd)	81g (2⅞oz)/ 170m (186yd)	90g (3¼oz)/ 189m (206½yd)	95g (3⅜oz)/ 200m (218¾yd)
Yarn E	49g (1¾oz)/ 103m (112½yd)	55g (2oz)/ 116m (126¾yd)	61g (2⅛oz)/ 128m (140yd)	69g (2½oz)/ 145m (158½yd)	75g (2⅝oz)/ 158m (172¾yd)	81g (2⅞oz)/ 170m (186yd)	90g (3¼oz)/ 189m (206½yd)	95g (3⅜oz)/ 200m (218¾yd)

SIZING CHART: NO EASE – GARMENT IS THE SAME SIZE AS BUST

	XS	S	M	L	XL	2XL	3XL	4XL
Bust	75cm (29½in)	85cm (33½in)	95cm (37⅜in)	105cm (41⅜in)	115cm (45¼in)	125cm (49¼in)	135cm (53⅛in)	145cm (57⅛in)
Garment circumference	75cm (29½in)	85cm (33½in)	95cm (37⅜in)	105cm (41⅜in)	115cm (45¼in)	125cm (49¼in)	135cm (53⅛in)	145cm (57⅛in)
Garment width	37.5cm (14¾in)	42.5cm (16¾in)	47.5cm (18¾in)	52.5cm (20⅝in)	57.5cm (22⅝in)	62.5cm (24⅝in)	67.5cm (26⅝in)	72.5cm (28½in)
Garment length	51cm (20⅛in)	52cm (20½in)	53cm (20⅞in)	54cm (21¼in)	55cm (21¾in)	56cm (22in)	57cm (22½in)	58cm (22⅞in)

Construction

This pattern is worked in two panels and seamed at the side and shoulders. By using an odd number of colours, you can float your yarns up the side to avoid weaving in lots of ends (see Taking It Further for more details on this). To shorten or lengthen, remove/add rows in multiples of two before the armhole section. Note: the armholes are deep to accommodate full sleeves.

Back

Set up round: Using yarn A and a 4.5mm (7) hook, 53 (59, 65, 74, 80, 86, 95, 101) fdc.

Alternatively, 54 (60, 66, 75, 81, 87, 96, 102) ch, 1dc in second ch from hook, 1dc in each ch to end, fasten off or float yarn, turn. 53 (59, 65, 74, 80, 86, 95, 101) dc.

In the next row you are going to work groups of 3tr over the dc sts and into the bottom ch.

R1 (rs): Attach yarn B to top of first dc, 3ch (counts as first tr here and throughout), miss 1 ch, 3tr in next ch, *miss 2 chs, 3tr in next ch, rep from * to last 2 ch, miss 1 ch, 1tr in last ch, fasten off or float yarn, turn. 17 (19, 21, 24, 26, 28, 31, 33) 3tr groups.

For the remainder of the vest, continue to follow yarn colours in pattern: A, B, C, D, E. At the end of each row, fasten off or float yarn before turning.

R2: Attach yarn C in top of first tr, 3ch, 1tr in same sp, 3tr in each sp to last sp, 1tr in last sp, 1tr in top of 3ch, turn. 16 (18, 20, 23, 25, 27, 30, 32) 3tr groups.

R3: Attach yarn D in top of first tr, 3ch, 3tr in each sp to end, 1tr in top of 3ch, turn.

R2 and R3 form pattern. Rep pattern following the colour order until you have 27 rows in total.

ARMHOLE SHAPING

R28: Attach yarn D into sp after first (first, second, second, third, third, fourth, fourth) 3tr group. 3ch, 1tr in same sp, 3tr in each of next 14 (16, 16, 19, 19, 21, 22, 24) sps, 2tr in next sp, turn.

R29: Attach next yarn colour in top of first tr, 3ch, 3tr in each of next 15 (17, 17, 20, 20, 22, 23, 25) sps, 1tr in top of 3ch, turn.

R30: Attach next yarn colour in top of first tr, 3ch, 1tr in same sp, 3tr in each of next 14 (16, 16, 19, 19, 21, 22, 24) sps, 1tr in last sp, 1tr in top of 3ch, turn.

R31: Attach next yarn colour in sp between 2tr and 3tr group, 3ch, 1tr in same sp, 3tr in each of next 13 (15, 15, 18, 18, 20, 21, 23) sps, 2tr in next sp, turn.

R32: Attach next yarn colour in top of first tr, 3ch, 3tr in each of next 14 (16, 16, 19, 19, 21, 22, 24) sps, 1tr in top of 3ch, turn.

R33: Attach next yarn colour in top of first tr, 3ch, 1tr in same sp, 3tr in each of next 13 (15, 15, 18, 18, 20, 21, 23) sps, 1tr in last sp, 1tr in top of 3ch, turn.

Sizes XS (S, M, L, XL) only:

R34–R35: Rep R32-33.

R36: Attach next yarn colour in sp between 2tr and 3tr group, 3ch, 1tr in same sp, 3tr in each of next 12 (14, 14, 17, 17) sps, 2tr in next sp, turn.

R37: Attach next yarn colour in top of first tr, 3ch, 3tr in each of next 13 (15, 15, 18, 18) sps, 1tr in top of 3ch, turn.

R38: Attach next yarn colour in top of first tr, 3ch, 1tr in same sp, 3tr in each of next 12 (14, 14, 17, 17) sps, 1tr in last sp, 1tr in top of 3ch, turn.

R37 and R38 form pattern. Repeat pattern 6 (6, 7, 7, 8) times.

Sizes S and L only: Rep R37 once more.

Sizes 2XL (3XL, 4XL) only:

R34: Attach next yarn colour in sp between 2tr and 3tr group, 3ch, 1tr in same sp, 3tr in each of next 19 (20, 22) sps, 2tr in next sp, turn.

R35: Attach next yarn colour in top of first tr, 3ch, 3tr in each of next 20 (21, 23) sps, 1tr in top of 3ch, turn.

R36: Attach next yarn colour in top of first tr, 3ch, 1tr in same sp, 3tr in each of next 19 (20, 22) sps, 1tr in last sp, 1tr in top of 3ch, turn.

R37: Attach next yarn colour in sp between 2tr and 3tr group, 3ch, 1tr in same sp, 3tr in each of next 18 (19, 21) sps, 2tr in next sp, turn.

R38: Attach next yarn colour in top of first tr, 3ch, 3tr in each of next 19 (20, 22) sps, 1tr in top of 3ch, turn.

R39: Attach next yarn colour in top of first tr, 3ch, 1tr in same sp, 3tr in each of next 18 (19, 21) sps, 1tr in last sp, 1tr in top of 3ch, turn.

R40: Attach next yarn colour in sp between 2tr and 3tr group, 3ch, 1tr in same sp, 3tr in each of next 17 (18, 20) sps, 2tr in next sp, turn.

R41: Attach next yarn colour in top of first tr, 3ch, 3tr in each of next 18 (19, 21) sps, 1tr in top of 3ch, turn.

R42: Attach next yarn colour in top of first tr, 3ch, 1tr in same sp, 3tr in each of next 17 (18, 20) sps, 1tr in last sp, 1tr in top of 3ch, turn.

Sizes 2XL (3XL) only: R41 and R42 form pattern. Rep pattern 6 (7) times.

Size 2XL only: Rep R41 once more.

Size 4XL only:

R43: Attach next yarn colour in sp between 2tr and 3tr group, 3ch, 1tr in same sp, 3tr in each of next 19 sps, 2tr in next sp, turn.

R44: Attach next yarn colour in top of last tr, 3ch, 3tr in each of next 20 sps, 1tr in top of 3ch, turn.

R45: Attach next yarn colour in top of last tr, 3ch, 1tr in same sp, 3tr in each of next 19 sps, 1tr in last sp, 1tr in top of 3ch, turn.

R46: Attach next yarn colour in sp between 2tr and 3tr group, 3ch, 1tr in same sp, 3tr in each of next 18 sps, 2tr in next sp, turn.

R47: Attach next yarn colour in top of last tr, 3ch, 3tr in each of next 19 sps, 1tr in top of 3ch, turn.

R48: Attach next yarn colour in top of last tr, 3ch, 1tr in same sp, 3tr in each of next 18 sps, 1tr in last sp, 1tr in top of 3ch, turn.

R47 and R48 form pattern. Rep pattern 4 times. Rep R47 once more.

Final row sizes XS, M, XL and 3XL only:

Attach next yarn colour in top of last tr, 3ch, 3tr in each of next 2 (x, 3, x, 4, x, 4, x) sps, 1tr in middle tr of next group, fasten off. With same side still facing, count 9 (x, 9, x, 10, x, 11, x) sps across and attach same colour yarn in middle tr of next group. 3ch, 3tr in each of next 2 (x, 3, x, 4, x, 4, x) sps, 1tr in top of 3ch, fasten off.

Final row sizes S, L, 2XL and 4XL only:

Attach next yarn colour in top of last tr, 3ch, 1tr in same sp, 3tr in each of next x (2, x, 3, x, 3, x, 3) sps, 2tr in next sp, fasten off. With same side still facing, count x (9, x, 10, x, 10, x, 11) sps across and attach same colour yarn in sp. 3ch, 1tr in same sp, 3tr in each of next x (2, x, 3, x, 3, x, 3) sps, 1tr in last sp, 1tr in top of 3ch, fasten off.

51 (52, 53, 54, 55, 56, 57, 58) rows in total.

Front

Sizes XS (S, M, L, XL) only: Work as for the back until end of R38. R37 and R38 form pattern. Rep pattern 1 (1, 1, 2, 2) times. Rep R37 once more.

Sizes 2XL (3XL) only: Work as for the back until end of R42. Rep R41, R42, R41.

Size 4XL only: Work as for the back until end of R47.

41 (41, 41, 43, 43, 45, 45, 47) rows in total.

All sizes work as follows:

RIGHT NECK SHAPING

R1: Attach next yarn colour in top of first tr, 3ch, 1tr in same sp, 3tr in each of next 3 (4, 4, 5, 5, 5, 5, 5) sps, 2tr in next sp, turn.

R2: Attach next yarn colour in sp between 2tr and 3tr group, 3ch, 1tr in same sp, 3tr in each of next 3 (4, 4, 5, 5, 5, 5, 5) sps, 1tr in top of 3ch, turn.

R3: Attach next yarn colour in top of first tr, 3ch, 1tr in same sp, 3tr in each of next 2 (3, 3, 4, 4, 4, 4, 4) sps, 2tr in next sp, turn.

R4: Attach next colour yarn in sp between 2tr and 3tr group, 3ch, 1tr in same sp, 3tr in each of next 2 (3, 3, 4, 4, 4, 4, 4) sps, 1tr in top of 3ch, turn.

R5: Attach next yarn colour to top of first tr, 3ch, 1tr in same sp, 3tr in each of next 1 (2, 2, 3, 3, 3, 3, 3) sps, 2tr in next sp, turn.

R6: Attach next yarn colour in top of first tr, 3ch, 3tr in each of next 2 (3, 3, 4, 4, 4, 4, 4) sps, 1tr in top of 3ch, turn.

R7: Attach next yarn colour in top of first tr, 3ch, 1tr in same sp, 3tr in each of next 1 (2, 2, 3, 3, 3, 3, 3) sps, 1tr in last sp, 1tr in top of 3ch, turn.

R6 and R7 form pattern. Rep pattern 1 (2, 2, 2, 2, 2, 2, 1) times.

Sizes XS, M, XL and 3XL only: Rep R6 once more.

LEFT NECK SHAPING

R1: With ws facing, count 5 (5, 5, 6, 6, 6, 7, 7) sps across from end of R1 on opposite side and attach same colour yarn. 3ch, 1tr in same sp, 3tr in each of next 3 (4, 4, 5, 5, 5, 5) sps, 1tr in last sp, 1tr in top of 3ch, turn.

R2: Attach next yarn colour in top of first tr, 3ch, 3tr in each of next 3 (4, 4, 5, 5, 5, 5, 5) sps, 2tr in next sp, turn.

R3: Attach next yarn colour in sp between 2tr and 3tr group, 3ch, 1tr in same sp, 3tr in each of next 2 (3, 3, 4, 4, 4, 4, 4) sps, 1tr in last sp, 1tr in top of 3ch, turn.

R4: Attach next yarn colour in top of first tr, 3ch, 3tr in each of next 2 (3, 3, 4, 4, 4, 4, 4) sps, 2tr in next sp, turn.

R5: Attach next yarn colour in sp between 2tr and 3tr group, 3ch, 1tr in same sp, 3tr in each of next 1 (2, 2, 3, 3, 3, 3, 3) sps, 1tr in last sp, 1tr in top of 3ch, turn.

R6: Attach next yarn colour in top of first tr, 3ch, 3tr in each of next 2 (3, 3, 4, 4, 4, 4, 4) sps, 1tr in top of 3ch, turn.

R7: Attach next yarn colour in top of first tr, 3ch, 1tr in same sp, 3tr in each of next 1 (2, 2, 3, 3, 3, 3, 3) sps, 1tr in last sp, 1tr in top of 3ch, turn.

R6 and R7 form pattern. Rep pattern 1 (2, 2, 2, 2, 2, 2, 1) times.

Sizes XS, M, XL and 3XL only: Rep R6 once more.

Block your panels if desired, then with rs facing each other, sew up shoulder seams and side seams.

HEM RIB

R1: Using a 4mm (G/6) hook, with rs facing, attach yarn A to first ch of the starting ch. 6ch, 1dc in second ch from hook, (1ch missed does not count as stitch), 1dc in each of next 4 chs, sl st across next 2 chs along starting ch to anchor your rib to the body, turn.

R2: 1dc blo in next 5 sts, turn.

R3: 1ch, 1dc blo in next 5 sts, sl st across next 2 chs along starting ch, turn.

R2 and R3 form pattern. Rep pattern until you reach the end. Hold edges of rib with rs facing each other, sl st along edge to form a seam. Fasten off.

ARMHOLE RIB (WORK ALIKE FOR BOTH ARMHOLES)

With rs facing, attach yarn A to bottom of armhole. Using a 4.5mm (7) hook, sl st evenly all around the armhole, aiming for 5 sl sts every two rows.

R1: Using a 4mm (G/6) hook, 6ch, 1dc in second ch from hook (1ch missed does not count as stitch), 1dc in each of next 4 chs, sl st blo across next 2 sl sts around armhole to anchor your rib, turn. Note: On curved sections of armhole, use 3 sl sts to anchor your rib.

R2: 1dc blo in next 5 sts, turn.

R3: 1ch, 1dc blo in next 5 sts, sl st across next 2 sl sts around armhole, turn.

R2 and R3 form pattern. Rep pattern until you reach the end. Hold edges of rib with rs facing each other, sl st along edge to form a seam. Fasten off.

NECK RIB

With rs facing, attach yarn A to side seam. Using a 4.5mm (7) hook, sl st evenly all around the neck, aiming for 5 sl sts every two rows.

R1: Using a 4mm (G/6) hook, 6ch, 1dc in second ch from hook (1ch missed does not count as stitch), 1dc in each of next 4 chs, sl st across next 2 sl sts around neck to anchor your rib, turn. Note: On the curves you may need to sl st across 3 sl sts to tighten your rib and prevent it from looking wavy.

R2: 1dc blo in next 5 sts, turn.

R3: 1ch, 1dc blo in next 5 sts, sl st across next 2 sl sts around neck, turn.

R2 and R3 form pattern. Rep pattern until you reach the end. Hold edges of rib with rs facing each other, sl st along edge to form a seam. Fasten off and weave in all ends.

Patchwork Jumper

Pick your four favourite colours and go to town with this stylish patchwork-effect jumper. This simple, boxy style with minimal shaping allows the colours to do the talking.

◇ **YOU WILL NEED**

Hook: 4mm (G/6)

Scissors

Yarn needle

Yarn: Sirdar Snuggly Double Knitting. 55% Nylon, 45% Acrylic, 50g (1¾oz) = 165m (180½yd), in the following shades:

- Yarn A: Tree House 515
- Yarn B: Cherry Pie 484
- Yarn C: Rosebud 510
- Yarn D: Tangerine 489

◇ **PATTERN NOTES**

Yarn weight: DK

Tension: 5 x 3tr groups and 11 rows = 10cm (4in)

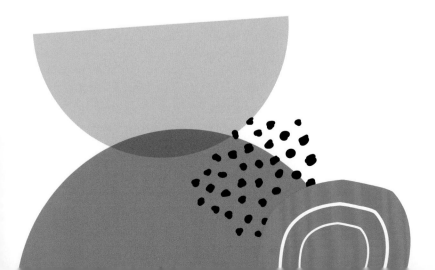

Patchwork Jumper Schematic

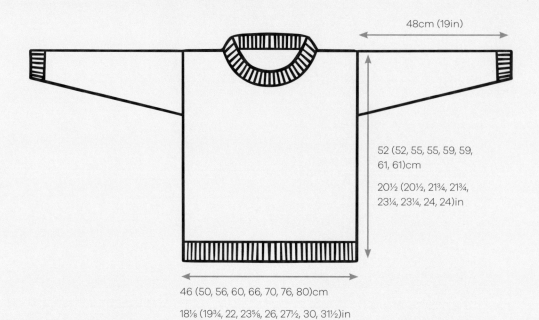

48cm (19in)

52 (52, 55, 55, 59, 59, 61, 61)cm

20½ (20½, 21¾, 21¾, 23¼, 23¼, 24, 24)in

46 (50, 56, 60, 66, 70, 76, 80)cm

18⅛ (19¾, 22, 23⅝, 26, 27½, 30, 31½)in

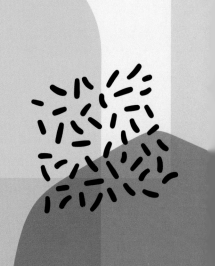

Yardage and Sizing

YARN QUANTITIES:

	XS	S	M	L	XL	2XL	3XL	4XL
Yarn A	123g (4¼oz)/ 406m (444yd)	133g (4¾oz)/ 439m (480yd)	154g (5½oz)/ 508m (555½yd)	165g (5¾oz)/ 545m (596yd)	179g (6¼oz)/ 591m (646¼yd)	185g (6½oz)/ 611m (668¼yd)	210g (7½oz)/ 693m (757¾yd)	222g (7¾oz)/ 733m (801½yd)
Yarn B	95g (3⅜oz)/ 314m (343½yd)	102g (3⅝oz)/ 337m (368½yd)	118g (4¼oz)/ 389m (425½yd)	126g (4½oz)/ 416m (455yd)	136g (4¾oz)/ 449m (491yd)	141g (5oz)/ 465m (508½yd)	160g (5⅝oz)/ 528m (577½yd)	170g (6oz)/ 561m (613½yd)
Yarn C	92g (3¼oz)/ 304m (332½yd)	100g (3½oz)/ 330m (361yd)	114g (4⅛oz)/ 376m (411¼yd)	121g (4⅜oz)/ 399m (436½yd)	131g (4½oz)/ 432m (472½yd)	136g (4¾oz)/ 449m (491yd)	153g (5⅜oz)/ 505m (552¼yd)	161g (5⅝oz)/ 531m (580¾yd)
Yarn D	92g (3¼oz)/ 304m (332½yd)	98g (3½oz)/ 323m (353¼yd)	111g (4oz)/ 366m (400¼yd)	116g (4⅛oz)/ 383m (419yd)	127g (4½oz)/ 419m (458¼yd)	132g (4⅝oz)/ 434m (474¾yd)	147g (5¼oz)/ 485m (530½yd)	154g (5½oz)/ 508m (555½yd)

SIZING CHART: 15-17CM (6–6¾IN) POSITIVE EASE DEPENDING ON SIZE

	XS	S	M	L	XL	2XL	3XL	4XL
Bust	75cm (29½in)	85cm (33½in)	95cm (37⅜in)	105cm (41⅜in)	115cm (45¼in)	125cm (49¼in)	135cm (53⅛in)	145cm (57⅛in)
Garment circumference	92cm (36¼in)	100cm (39⅜in)	112cm (44in)	120cm (47¼in)	132cm (52in)	140cm (55⅛in)	152cm (59¾in)	160cm (63in)
Garment width	46cm (18⅛in)	50cm (19¾in)	56cm (22in)	60cm (23⅝in)	66cm (26in)	70cm (27½in)	76cm (30in)	80cm (31½in)
Garment length	52cm (20½in)	52cm (20½in)	55cm (21¾in)	55cm (21¾in)	59cm (23¼in)	59cm (23¼in)	61cm (24in)	61cm (24in)
Sleeve length	48cm (19in)	48cm (19in)	48cm (19in)	48cm (19in)	48cm (19in)	48cm (19in)	48cm (19in)	48cm (19in)

Construction

This jumper is worked in two separate panels and seamed together at the sides and shoulders. The sleeves are worked in the round from cuff to bicep. To lengthen or shorten the jumper, add or remove 2 (or 4) rows in the lower section and 2 (or 4) rows in the upper section, to keep the design central.

Back

BACK LOWER SECTION

Set up round: Using yarn A, 71 (77, 86, 92, 101, 107, 116, 122) fdc.

Alternatively, 72 (78, 87, 93, 102, 108, 117, 123) ch. 1dc in second ch from hook, 1dc in each ch to end. 71 (77, 86, 92, 101, 107, 116, 122) sts. Fasten off.

On the next row you are going to work groups of 3tr over the dc sts and into the bottom ch. When changing colours mid row, always drop the old colour to the ws of the work.

R1 (rs): Using yarn B, 3ch in top of first st, (counts as first tr here and throughout), miss 1 ch, [3tr in next ch, miss 2 chs] 12 (13, 14, 15, 17, 18, 19, 20) times, drop yarn B and using yarn A [3tr in next ch, miss 2 chs] 10 (11, 13, 14, 15, 16, 18, 19) times, 3tr in next ch, miss 1 ch, 1tr in last ch, turn. 23 (25, 28, 30, 33, 35, 38, 40) groups.

R2: 3ch, 1tr in same sp, [3tr in next sp] 11 (12, 13, 14, 16, 17, 18, 19) times, drop yarn A and using yarn B [3tr in next sp] 11 (12, 14, 15, 16, 17, 19, 20) times, 1tr in last sp, 1tr in top of 3ch, turn. 22 (24, 27, 29, 32, 34, 37, 39) groups.

R3: 3ch, [3tr in next sp] 12 (13, 14, 15, 17, 18, 19, 20) times, drop yarn B and using yarn A [3tr in next sp] 11 (12, 14, 15, 16, 17, 19, 20) times, 1tr in top of 3ch, turn.

R2 and R3 form pattern. Rep pattern 10 (10, 11, 11, 12, 12, 13, 13) more times.

Rep R2 once more. Fasten off yarn A. 24 (24, 26, 26, 28, 28, 30, 30) rows.

BACK MIDDLE SECTION

R1: 3ch, [3tr in next sp] 12 (13, 14, 15, 17, 18, 19, 20) times, drop yarn B and using yarn C [3tr in next sp] 11 (12, 14, 15, 16, 17, 19, 20) times, 1tr in top of 3ch, turn.

R2: 3ch, 1tr in same sp, [3tr in next sp] 11 (12, 13, 14, 16, 17, 18, 19) times, drop yarn C and using yarn B [3tr in next sp] 11 (12, 14, 15, 16, 17, 19, 20) times, 1tr in top of 3ch, turn.

R1 and R2 form pattern. Rep pattern 2 more times. Fasten off yarn B. 30 (30, 32, 32, 34, 34, 36, 36) rows.

BACK UPPER SECTION

R1: Using yarn D, 3ch, [3tr in next sp] 12 (13, 14, 15, 17, 18, 19, 20) times, drop yarn D and using yarn C [3tr in next sp] 11 (12, 14, 15, 16, 17, 19, 20) times, 1tr in top of 3ch, turn.

R2: 3ch, 1tr in same sp, [3tr in next sp] 11 (12, 13, 14, 16, 17, 18, 19) times, drop yarn C and using yarn D [3tr in next sp] 11 (12, 14, 15, 16, 17, 19, 20) times, 1tr in last sp, 1tr in top of 3ch, turn.

R1 and R2 form pattern. Rep pattern 11 (11, 12, 12, 13, 13, 14, 14) more times. Fasten off both colours. 54 (54, 58, 58, 62, 62, 66, 66) rows.

Front

FRONT LOWER SECTION

Work as for the Back Lower Section to end of set up round, turn. Do not fasten off yarn A.

On the next row you are going to work groups of 3tr over the dc sts and into the bottom ch.

R1 (rs): 3ch, miss 1 ch, [3tr in next ch, miss 2 chs] 11 (12, 14, 15, 16, 17, 19, 20) times, drop yarn A and using yarn B [3tr in next ch, miss 2 chs] 11 (12, 13, 14, 16, 17, 18, 19) times, 3tr in next ch, miss 1 ch, 1tr in last ch, turn. 23 (25, 28, 30, 33, 35, 38, 40) groups.

R2: 3ch, 1tr in same sp, [3tr in next sp] 11 (12, 14, 15, 16, 17, 19, 20) times, drop yarn B and using yarn A [3tr in next sp] 11 (12, 13, 14, 16, 17, 18, 19) times, 1tr in last sp, 1tr in top of 3ch, turn. 22 (24, 27, 29, 32, 34, 37, 39) groups.

R3: 3ch, [3tr in next sp] 11 (12, 14, 15, 16, 17, 19, 20) times, drop yarn A and using yarn B [3tr in next sp] 12 (13, 14, 15, 17, 18, 19, 20) times, 1tr in top of 3ch, turn.

R2 and R3 form pattern. Rep pattern 10 (10, 11, 11, 12, 12, 13, 13) more times.

Rep R2 once more. Fasten off yarn A. 24 (24, 26, 26, 28, 28, 30, 30) rows.

FRONT MIDDLE SECTION

R1: Using yarn C, 3ch, [3tr in next sp] 11 (12, 14, 15, 16, 17, 19, 20) times, drop yarn C and using yarn B [3tr in next sp] 12 (13, 14, 15, 17, 18, 19, 20) times, 1tr in top of 3ch, turn.

R2: 3ch, 1tr in same sp, [3tr in next sp] 11 (12, 14, 15, 16, 17, 19, 20) times, drop yarn B and using yarn C [3tr in next sp] 11 (12, 13, 14, 16, 17, 18, 19) times, 1tr in last sp, 1tr in top of 3ch, turn.

R1 and R2 form pattern. Rep pattern 2 more times. Fasten off yarn B. 30 (30, 32, 32, 34, 34, 36, 36) rows.

FRONT UPPER SECTION

R1: Using yarn C, 3ch, [3tr in next sp] 11 (12, 14, 15, 16, 17, 19, 20) times, drop yarn C and using yarn D [3tr in next sp] 12 (13, 14, 15, 17, 18, 19, 20) times, 1tr in top of 3ch, turn.

R2: 3ch, 1tr in same sp, [3tr in next sp] 11 (12, 14, 15, 16, 17, 19, 20) times, drop yarn D and using yarn C [3tr in next sp] 11 (12, 13, 14, 16, 17, 18, 19) times, 1tr in last sp, 1tr in top of 3ch, turn.

R1 and R2 form pattern. Rep pattern 5 (5, 5, 5, 6, 6, 6, 6) more times. 42 (42, 44, 44, 48, 48, 50, 50) rows.

LEFT SHOULDER SHAPING

R1: 3ch, 3tr in next 7 (8, 10, 11, 12, 13, 15, 16) sps, 2tr in next sp, turn.

R2: Sl st into first st, sl st into sp between 2tr and 3tr group, 3ch, 1tr in same sp, 3tr in each of next 6 (7, 9, 10, 11, 12, 14, 15) sps, 1tr in last sp, 1tr in top of 3ch, turn.

R3: 3ch, 3tr in next 6 (7, 9, 10, 11, 12, 14, 15) sps, 2tr in next sp, turn.

R4: Sl st into first st, sl st into sp between 2tr and 3tr group, 3ch, 1tr in same sp, 3tr in each of next 5 (6, 8, 9, 10, 11, 13, 14) sps, 1tr in last sp, 1tr in top of 3ch, turn.

Sizes XS and S only: Work from R7.

All other sizes:

R5: 3ch, 3tr in next x (x, 8, 9, 10, 11, 13, 14) sps, 2tr in next sp, turn.

R6: Sl st into first st, sl st into sp between 2tr and 3tr group, 3ch, 1tr in same sp, 3tr in each of next x (x, 7, 8, 9, 10, 12, 13) sps, 1tr in last sp, 1tr in top of 3ch, turn.

R7: 3ch, 3tr in next 6 (7, 8, 9, 10, 11, 13, 14) sps, 1tr in top of 3ch, turn.

R8: 3ch, 1tr in same sp, 3tr in next 5 (6, 7, 8, 9, 10, 12, 13) sps, 1tr in last sp, 1tr in top of 3ch, turn.

R7 and R8 form pattern. Rep pattern 3 (3, 3, 3, 3, 3, 4, 4) more times. Fasten off. 54 (54, 58, 58, 62, 62, 66, 66) rows.

RIGHT SHOULDER SHAPING

With rs facing, count 8 (8, 7, 7, 8, 8, 7, 7) sps along from end of Left Shoulder Shaping R1 and attach yarn D into sp.

R1: 3ch, 1tr in same sp, 3tr in next 7 (8, 10, 11, 12, 13, 15, 16) sps, 1tr in top of 3ch, turn.

R2: 3ch, 1tr in same sp, 3tr in next 6 (7, 9, 10, 11, 12, 14, 15) sps, 2tr in next sp, turn.

R3: Sl st into first st, sl st into sp between 2tr and 3tr group, 3ch, 1tr in same sp, 3tr in each of next 6 (7, 9, 10, 11, 12, 14, 15) sps, 1tr in top of 3ch, turn.

R4: 3ch, 1tr in same sp, 3tr in next 5 (6, 8, 9, 10, 11, 13, 14) sps, 2tr in next sp, turn.

Sizes XS and S only: Work from R7.

All other sizes:

R5: Sl st into first st, sl st into sp between 2tr and 3tr group, 3ch, 1tr in same sp, 3tr in each of next x (x, 8, 9, 10, 11, 13, 14) sps, 1tr in top of 3ch, turn.

R6: 3ch, 1tr in same sp, 3tr in each of next x (x, 7, 8, 9, 10, 12, 13) sps, 2tr in next sp, turn.

R7: 3ch, 3tr in next 6 (7, 8, 9, 10, 11, 13, 14) sps, 1tr in top of 3ch, turn.

R8: 3ch, 1tr in same sp, 3tr in next 5 (6, 7, 8, 9, 10, 12, 13) sps, 1tr in last sp, 1tr in top of 3ch, turn.

R7 and R8 form pattern. Rep pattern 3 (3, 3, 3, 3, 3, 4, 4) more times. Fasten off. 54 (54, 58, 58, 62, 62, 66, 66) rows.

LEFT SLEEVE

Work in yarn A until end of R25, Fasten off yarn A and work R26 onwards in yarn C.

If you wish to add or remove rounds from the sleeves, always do so in multiples of 2 rounds. Remember to change colour at the new halfway point.

Set up round: Using yarn A, 36 (36, 39, 39, 42, 42, 45, 45) fdc.

Alternatively, ch the amount as above and join to first ch with a sl st to form a circle. 1ch, 1dc in each ch to end, join to top of first dc with a sl st. 36 (36, 39, 39, 42, 42, 45, 45) sts.

On the next row you are going to work groups of 3tr over the dc sts and into the bottom ch.

R1 (rs): 3ch, 2tr in same ch, miss 2 chs, [3tr in next ch, miss 2 chs] 11 (11, 12, 12, 13, 13, 14, 14) times, join to top of 3ch with a sl st, turn. 12 (12, 13, 13, 14, 14, 15, 15) groups.

Sizes 2XL–4XL only: Skip R2 – go to increase rounds.

R2: 3ch, 2tr in same sp, 3tr in each sp to end, join to top of 3ch with a sl st, turn.

All sizes: Rep R2 4 (1, 1, 1, 1, x, x, x) times.

Work the following two increase rounds:

Increase R1: 3ch, 2tr in same sp, [3tr in next sp] until you reach the centre of the round (or as near as possible to) 4tr in next sp, [3tr in next sp] to end, join to top of 3ch with a sl st, turn.

Increase R2: 3ch, 2tr in same sp, [3tr in next sp] until you reach the 4tr group, 3tr in between the second and third tr of the 4tr group, [3tr in next sp] to end, join to top of 3ch with a sl st, turn. You will have increased by one 3tr group.

Size XS only: (Rep R2 7 times followed by the two increase rounds) 4 times, rep R2 6 times, fasten off. 50 rounds.

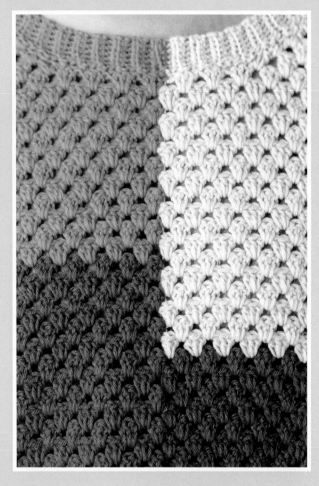

Sizes S and M only: (Rep R2 5 times followed by the two increase rounds) 6 times, rep R2 3 times, fasten off. 50 rounds.

Sizes L and XL only: (Rep R2 3 times, followed by the two increase rounds) 4 times, (rep R2 5 times followed by the two increase rounds) 3 times, rep R2 4 times, fasten off. 50 rounds.

Size 2XL only: (Work R2 3 times followed by the two increase rounds) 9 times, rep R2 3 times, fasten off. 50 rounds.

Size 3XL only: (Work R2 followed by the two increase rounds) 3 times, (Rep R2 3 times followed by the two increase rounds) 7 times, rep R2 3 times, fasten off. 50 rounds.

Size 4XL only: (Work R2 followed by the two increase rounds) 8 times, (rep R2 3 times followed by the two increase rounds) 4 times, rep R2 3 times, fasten off. 50 rounds.

RIGHT SLEEVE

Work as Left Sleeve but using yarn B until end of R25. Fasten off yarn B and work R26 onwards in yarn D.

Block your panels if desired, then with rs facing each other, sew up shoulder seams. Sew top of each sleeve along edge of body. Sew up side seams.

HEM RIB

R1: With rs of front facing, attach yarn A to first ch at side seam. 7ch, 1dc in second ch from hook, (1ch missed does not count as stitch), 1dc in each of next 5 chs, sl st across next 2 chs along starting ch to anchor your rib to the body, turn.

R2: 1dc blo in next 6 sts, turn.

R3: 1ch, 1dc blo in next 6 sts, sl st across next 2 chs along starting ch, turn.

R2 and R3 form pattern. Rep pattern until you reach the opposite side seam, fasten off.

Rep from R1 on back, leaving front and back hem rib unattached at side seams.

TIP

REMEMBER THAT ON THE BACK THE COLOURS WILL BE ON OPPOSITE SIDES TO THE FRONT, TO ENSURE THE SAME COLOURS MEET AT THE SIDE SEAMS.

CUFF RIB

Work as Hem Rib, using yarn A for left sleeve and yarn B for right sleeve. Work all the way around the cuff and seam edges together on ws using sl st.

NECK RIB

With rs facing, attach yarn C to centre back and sl st around the yarn C section of neckline, change to yarn D at centre front, sl st around the yarn D section of neckline, aiming for 2 sl sts per row. Fasten off both colours.

R1: Reattach yarn C under first sl st at centre back, 7ch, 1dc in second ch from hook (1ch missed does not count as stitch), 1dc in each of next 5 chs, sl st across next 2 sl sts around neckline to anchor your rib, turn.

Note: On the curves you may need to sl st across 3 sl sts to tighten your rib and prevent it from looking wavy.

R2: 1dc blo in next 6 sts, turn.

R3: 1ch, 1dc blo in next 6 sts, sl st across next 2 sl sts around neckline, turn.

R2 and R3 form pattern. Rep pattern until you reach centre front colour change, drop yarn C and work remaining rib in yarn D to end. Hold edges of rib with rs facing each other, sl st along edge to form a seam. Fasten off and weave in all ends.

Chevron Vest

Grab some summery colours and whip up this flattering cotton vest top with playful chevron accents. Made using 4ply cotton, it comes with customizable options to achieve the perfect fit.

✧ YOU WILL NEED

Hook: 3mm (D)

Scissors

Yarn needle

Yarn: Scheepjes Cotton 8. 100% Cotton, 50g (1¾oz) = 170m (186yd), in the following shades:

- Yarn A: 715 (skin)
- Yarn B: 720 (fuchsia)
- Yarn C: 716 (orange)

✧ PATTERN NOTES

Yarn weight: 4 ply (fingering)

Tension: 5.5 x 3tr groups and 11 rows = 10cm (4in)

To check your tension, work the triangle for the front until you have six rows. Your triangle should measure 15.5cm (6⅛in) wide and 8cm (3⅛in) high.

Chevron Vest Schematic

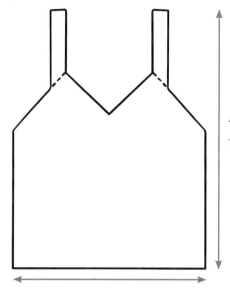

48 (51, 51, 52, 52, 54, 54, 55)cm

19 (20⅛, 20⅛, 20½, 20½, 21¼, 21¼, 21¾)in

32 (37, 42, 47, 52, 57, 62, 68)cm

12⅝ (14½, 16½, 18½, 20½, 22½, 24⅜, 26¾)in

Yardage and Sizing

YARN QUANTITIES:

	XS	S	M	L	XL	2XL	3XL	4XL
Yarn A	95g (3⅜oz)/ 332m (363⅛yd)	119g (4¼oz)/ 405m (443yd)	136g (4¾oz)/ 462m (505¼yd)	163g (5¾oz)/ 554m (606yd)	181g (6⅜oz)/ 616m (673¾yd)	211g (7¾oz)/ 718m (785¼yd)	230g (8½oz)/ 782m (855¼yd)	264g (9⅜oz)/ 898m (982⅛yd)
Yarn B	13g (½oz) /44m (48⅛yd)	14g (½oz) /48m (52½yd)	15g (½oz) /51m (55¾yd)	17g (⅝oz) /58m (63½yd)	19g (⅝oz) /65m (71⅛yd)	21g (¾oz) /71m (77⅝yd)	22g (¾oz) /75m (82yd)	25g (⅞oz) /85m (93yd)
Yarn C	13g (½oz) /44m (48⅛yd)	14g (½oz) /48m (52½yd)	15g (½oz) /51m (55¾yd)	17g (⅝oz) /58m (63½yd)	19g (⅝oz) /65m (71⅛yd)	21g (¾oz) /71m (77⅝yd)	22g (¾oz) / 5m (82yd)	25g (⅞oz) /85m (93yd)

SIZING CHART 9-11CM (3½–4¼IN) POSITIVE EASE DEPENDING ON SIZE

	XS	S	M	L	XL	2XL	3XL	4XL
Bust	75cm (29½in)	85cm (33½in)	95cm (37⅜in)	105cm (41⅜in)	115cm (45¼in)	125cm (49¼in)	135cm (53⅛in)	145cm (57⅛in)
Garment circumference	64cm (25¼in)	74cm (29⅛in)	84cm (33⅛in)	94cm (37in)	104cm (41in)	114cm (44⅞in)	124cm (48¾in)	136cm (53½in)
Garment width	32cm (12⅝in)	37cm (14½in)	42cm (16½in)	47cm (18½in)	52cm (20½in)	57cm (22½in)	62cm (24⅜in)	68cm (26¾in)
Garment length	48cm (19in)	51cm (20⅛in)	51cm (20⅛in)	52cm (20½in)	52cm (20½in)	54cm (21¼in)	54cm (21¼in)	55cm (21¾in)

Construction

The front and back are worked in two separate panels and seamed at the sides. The straps are worked onto the front and back in two halves and seamed at the shoulder. There are several customizable options to achieve the perfect fit. You can extend the outer edges for more coverage and continue into the straps or go straight to the straps and fill in the underarms. To extend the body, add rows in multiples of 7 (2 striped rows and 5 main colour rows).

Front

R1: Using yarn A and a 3mm (D) hook, 3ch. Sl st to first ch to form a circle. 3ch, (3tr, 3ch, 4tr) in centre of circle, turn.

R2: 3ch, 3tr in sp between first and second tr, (3tr, 3ch, 3tr) in 3ch sp, 4tr in sp between third and fourth tr, turn.

R3: 3ch, 3tr in sp between first and second tr, 3tr in next sp, (3tr, 3ch, 3tr) in 3ch sp, 3tr in next sp, 4tr in sp between third and fourth tr, turn.

R4: 3ch, 3tr in sp between first and second tr, 3tr in each sp to 3ch sp, (3tr, 3ch, 3tr) in 3ch sp, 3tr in each sp to end, 4tr in sp between third and fourth tr, turn.

Rep R4 until you have 6 (7, 7, 8, 8, 8, 9) rows. You will have 6 (7, 7, 8, 8, 8, 9) 3tr groups along each side. Place a st marker in the last loop and fasten off leaving a 15cm (6in) tail.

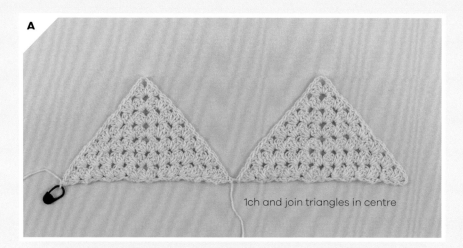

1ch and join triangles in centre

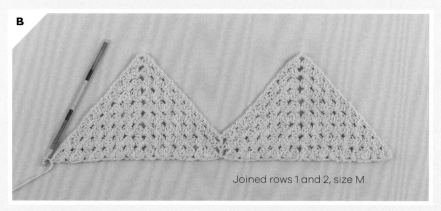

Joined rows 1 and 2, size M

Make a second identical triangle, place a st marker in last loop but do not fasten off.

Place both triangles side by side with the same sides facing up and the 15cm (6in) yarn tail in the centre. Using the yarn tail, 1ch and join with a sl st to top of 3ch on second triangle, so they are joined in the centre. Remove st marker on second triangle, insert hook and turn (A).

Sizes XS (S) only:

Joined R1: 3ch, *3tr in next 5(6) sps, (3tr, 3ch, 3tr) in 3ch sp, 3tr in next 5(6) sps**, 1tr in 1ch between triangles, rep from * to **, 1tr in top of 3ch, turn. You will have 6 (7) 3tr groups on each outer edge, 6 (7) 3tr groups on each inner edge, 24 (28) 3tr groups in the row.

Read Colour Changes section, then contine working from Main Body Row All Sizes.

Sizes M–4XL only:

Joined R1: 3ch, 3tr in sp between first and second tr, 3tr in each sp to 3ch sp, (3tr, 3ch, 3tr) in 3ch sp, 3tr in each sp to centre, 1tr in 1ch between triangles, 3tr in each sp to second 3ch sp, (3tr, 3ch, 3tr) in 3ch sp, 3tr in each sp to last sp, 4tr in sp between 3ch and tr of last group, turn. You will have x (x, 8, 9, 9, 9, 9, 10) 3tr groups on each outer edge, x (x, 7, 8, 8, 8, 8, 9) 3tr groups on each inner edge and x (x, 30, 34, 34, 34, 34, 38) 3tr groups in the row.

Joined R2: 3ch, 3tr in sp between first and second tr, 3tr in each sp to 3ch sp, (3tr, 3ch, 3tr) in 3ch sp, 3tr in each sp to centre, 1tr in top of 1tr, 3tr in each sp to second 3ch sp, (3tr, 3ch, 3tr) in 3ch sp, 3tr in each sp to last sp, 4tr in sp between 3ch and tr of last group, turn. You will have x (x, 9, 10, 10, 10, 10, 11) 3tr groups on each outer edge, x (x, 7, 8, 8, 8, 8, 9) 3tr groups on each inner edge and x (x, 32, 36, 36, 36, 36, 40) 3tr groups in the row (B).

Rep Joined R2 x (x, 0, 0, 2, 4, 6, 6) times.

Sizes 3XL and 4XL only: See note below about colour change for rows 15-17.

You will have x (x, 9, 10, 12, 14, 16, 17) 3tr groups on each outer edge, x (x, 7, 8, 8, 8, 8, 9) 3tr groups on each inner edge, x (x, 32, 36, 40, 44, 48, 52) 3tr groups in the row and x (x, 9, 10, 12, 14, 16, 17) rows in total.

All sizes: Read Colour Changes section, then continue working from Main Body Row All Sizes.

COLOUR CHANGES

Work a row of yarn B followed by a row of yarn C on the following rows only:

Size XS: Rows 9 and 10, 16 and 17, 23 and 24.

Sizes S and M: Rows 11 and 12, 18 and 19, 25 and 26.

Sizes L and XL: Rows 13 and 14, 20 and 21, 27 and 28.

Sizes 2XL and 3XL: Rows 15 and 16, 22 and 23, 29 and 30.

Size 4XL: Rows 17 and 18, 24 and 25, 31 and 32.

MAIN BODY ROW ALL SIZES

Main body row: 3ch, 3tr in each sp to 3ch sp, (3tr, 3ch, 3tr) in 3ch sp, 3tr in each sp to centre, 1tr in top of the 1tr, 3tr in each sp to second 3ch sp, (3tr, 3ch, 3tr) in 3ch sp, 3tr in each sp to last sp, 1tr in top of 3ch, turn. You will have 6 (7, 9, 10, 12, 14, 16, 17) 3tr groups on each outer edge, 6 (7, 7, 8, 8, 8, 8, 9) 3tr groups on each inner edge, 24 (28, 32, 36, 40, 44, 48, 52) 3tr groups in the row.

Rep main body row until you have 29 (31, 31, 33, 33, 35, 35, 37) rows in total. Fasten off.

Back

Work in the same way as the front.

JOIN SIDE SEAMS

With rs facing each other, sew the front to the back at the side seams.

Note for size XS only: This top has little stretch across the hem, so if your bust circumference is within 5cm (2in) of your waist circumference, you may wish to leave the last 3cm (1⅛in) of side seam open at the hem, for ease of getting on and off. When working your hem trim, work 3dc at the corners and continue the dc sts up and around the side openings.

Sizes XS–M only: Work from straps. If you prefer a higher underarm, follow the instructions for size L in the underarm shelf section after you have made your straps.

Sizes L–4XL only: At this stage, try on your vest. Depending on your upper chest circumference and shoulder width, you may wish to extend the outer edges to provide further coverage. To do this, work side extension row(s) as set out in the following instructions. If you skip the side extension rows, you will need to heighten the underarms by working the underarm shelf. Work straps first, then work underarm shelf.

SIDE EXTENSIONS: SIZES L (XL, 2XL, 3XL, 4XL) ONLY (C)

Note: You can work as many rows as necessary, the rows per size are guidelines only. These rows have decreases to taper the vest toward the underarm. These can be omitted if necessary – just work rows of 3tr groups as normal. However, extra decreases can be added along each row if further tapering is needed. These row(s) will also form the first row(s) of your straps.

R1: With ws facing you, attach yarn to 3ch sp at peak. 3ch, 3tr in 3ch sp, 3tr in next 4 (5, 6, 7, 7) sps, 2tr in next sp, 3tr in next 4 (5, 6, 7, 8) sps, 1tr in side seam, 3tr in next 4 (5, 6, 7, 8) sps on other side, 2tr in next sp, 3tr in next 4 (5, 6, 7, 7) sps to 3ch sp on other side, 4tr in sp, turn.

Size L only: Work from R2 of strap 1. Repeat side extension and strap 1 on opposite side. On remaining 2 peaks, count 2 sps down from top and attach yarn. Work from R2 of strap 2.

R2: 3ch, 3tr in sp between 1st and 2nd tr, 3tr in next x (5, 6, 7, 7) sps, miss next sp, 3tr in space between 2tr sts, miss next sp, 3tr in next x (4, 5, 6, 7) sps, 1tr in 1tr at side seam, 3tr in next x (4, 5, 6, 7) sps, miss next sp, 3tr in sp between 2tr sts, miss next sp, 3tr in next x (5, 6, 7, 7) sps, 4tr in sp between 3tr and tr of last group, turn.

Size XL only: You will have 11 groups down each edge. Work from R3 of strap 2. Repeat side extension rows and strap 2 on opposite side. On remaining 2 peaks, count 2 sps down from top and attach yarn. Work from R3 of strap 1.

R3: 3ch, 3tr in sp between first and second tr, 3tr in next x (x, 5, 6, 7) sps, 2tr in next sp, 3tr in next x (x, 6, 7, 7) sps, 1tr in 1tr at side seam, 3tr in next x (x, 6, 7, 7) sps on other side, 2tr in next sp, 3tr in next x (x, 5, 6, 7) sps, 4tr in sp between 3ch and tr of last group, turn.

Size 2XL only: You will have 13 groups down each edge. Work from R2 of strap 1. Repeat side extension R1 and strap 1 on opposite side. On remaining 2 peaks, count 2 sps down from top and attach yarn. Work from R2 of strap 2.

R4: 3ch, 3tr in sp between 1st and 2nd tr, 3tr in next x (x, x, 6, 7) sps, miss next sp, 3tr in sp in between the 2tr sts, miss next sp, 3tr in next x (x, x, 6, 6) sps, 1tr in 1tr at side seam, 3tr in next x (x, x, 6, 6) sps, miss next sp, 3tr in sp between 2tr sts, miss next sp, 3tr in next x (x, x, 6, 7) sps, 4tr in sp between 3ch and tr of last group, turn.

Size 3XL only: You will have 14 groups down each edge. Work from R3 of strap 2. Repeat side extension rows and strap 2 on opposite side. On remaining 2 peaks, count 3 sps down from top and attach yarn. Work from R3 of strap 1.

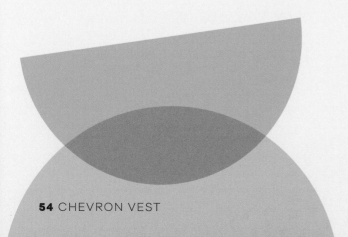

R5: 3ch, 3tr in sp between first and second tr, 3tr in next 6 sps, 2tr in next sp, 3tr in next 7 sps, 1tr in 1tr at side seam, 3tr in next 7 sps on other side, 2tr in next sp, 3tr in next 6 sps, 4tr in sp between 3ch and tr of last group, turn.

Size 4XL: You will have 15 groups down each edge. Work from R2 of strap 1. Repeat side extension R1 and strap 1 on opposite side. On remaining 2 peaks, count 3 sps down from 3ch sp and attach yarn. Work from R2 of strap 2.

You will have 1 (2, 3, 4, 5) side extension rows.

Strap 1

You will need to work 10, 11 or 12 rows for your strap, depending on whether your torso is short, medium, or long.

With ws of sts in last row facing, count 1 (2, 2, 2, 2, 3, 3) sps down from 3ch sp at peak and attach yarn.

R1: 3ch, 3tr in next 0 (1, 1, 1, 1, 2, 2) sps, 4tr in 3ch sp, turn.

R2: 3ch, 3tr in sp between first and second tr, 3tr in next 0 (1, 1, 1, 1, 2, 2) sps, 1tr in top of 3ch (if previous row is a side extension row, work 1tr in next sp instead), turn.

R3: 3ch, 3tr in next 0 (1, 1, 1, 1, 2, 2) sps, 4tr in sp between 3ch and tr, turn.

R2 and R3 form pattern. Alternate R2 and R3 until you have 10, 11 or 12 rows (including any side extension rows – see note at start of strap regarding length).

Square off strap:

Sizes S–4XL only: 3ch, 3tr in next x (1, 1, 1, 1, 2, 2) sps, 1tr in top of 3ch, turn.

Sizes 3XL–4XL only: 3ch, 3tr in next sp, 1tr in top of 3ch, turn.

All sizes: 2ch, 1tr in top of 3ch, fasten off.

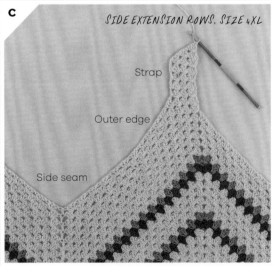

C

SIDE EXTENSION ROWS, SIZE 4XL

Strap

Outer edge

Side seam

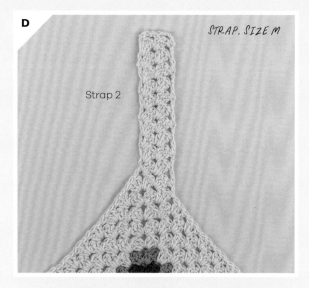

D

STRAP, SIZE M

Strap 2

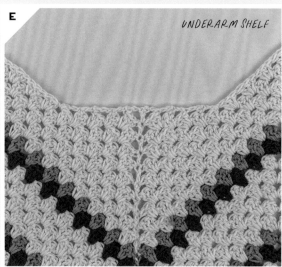

E

UNDERARM SHELF

TIP
IF YOU FIND THAT YOUR UNDERARM SHELF IS GAPING, TRY USING A 2.5MM (C12) HOOK FOR THIS SECTION, OR START EACH ROW WITH 2CH, AND ENDING WITH A HTR INSTEAD.

Strap 2

With ws of sts in last row facing, attach yarn in 3ch sp at peak.

R1: 3ch, 3tr in 3ch sp, 3tr in next 0 (1, 1, 1, 1, 1, 2, 2) sps, 1tr in next sp, turn.

R2: 3ch, 3tr in next 0 (1, 1, 1, 1, 1, 2, 2) sps, 4tr in sp between 3ch and tr, turn.

R3: 3ch, 3tr in sp between first and second tr, 3tr in next 0 (1, 1, 1, 1, 2, 2) sps, 1tr in top of 3ch, (if previous row is a side extension row, work 1tr in next sp instead), turn.

R2 and R3 form pattern. Alternate R2 and R3 until you have 10, 11 or 12 rows (including any side extension rows), depending on height (D).

Square off strap: Work as for strap 1.

Seam up both straps at shoulder.

UNDERARM SHELF (E)

Sizes L (XL, 2XL, 3XL ,4XL) only: You do not need to work your size for the shelf, you can work the instructions for any size depending on how much underarm you wish to fill in.

R1: With ws of sts in last row facing you, count 4 (5, 6, 7, 8) sps up from top of side seam and attach yarn. 3ch, 3tr in next 2 (3, 4, 5, 6) sps, 1tr in side seam, 3tr in next 2 (3, 4, 5, 6) sps on opposite side, 1tr in next sp, turn.

R2: 3ch, 3tr in next 1 (2, 3, 4, 5) sps, 1tr in top of 1tr at side seam, 3tr in next 1 (2, 3, 4, 5) sps on opposite side, 1tr in top of 3ch, turn. Size L only - go to last row.

R3: 3ch, 3tr in each sp to side seam, 1tr in 1tr at side seam, 3tr in each sp to end, 1tr in top of 3ch, turn.

Rep R3 x (0, 1, 2, 3) times.

Last row: 2ch, 1tr in 1tr at side seam, 1tr in top of 3ch, fasten off.

Repeat on opposite underarm.

Trim

Work each section with rs facing you.

Attach yarn to strap seam at shoulder. 1ch, work dc sts evenly around neckline, join to top of first dc with a sl st. Fasten off. Approx 5dc to 2 rows.

Attach yarn to side seam or centre of underarm shelf at underarm. (Tip – to tighten any gaping on underarm shelf, work 3dc to 2 rows across this section only.) 1ch, work dc sts evenly around armhole, join to top of first dc with a sl st. Fasten off. Repeat on opposite armhole.

Attach yarn to side seam at hem. 1ch, work dc sts evenly along bottom edge, join to top of first dc with a sl st. Fasten off. Weave in all ends and block to given dimensions.

Striped Cardigan

This oversized cardigan uses vertical granny stripes and a cotton blend yarn to create a summery layer for those warmer evenings. A transitional piece which looks great with jeans or shorts.

✧ YOU WILL NEED

Hook: 4mm (G/6)

Scissors

Yarn needle

Yarn: Scheepjes Softfun. 60% Cotton, 40% Acrylic, 50g (1¾oz) = 140m (153⅛yd), in the following shades:

- Yarn A: Orchid 2657
- Yarn B: Cantaloupe 2652

✧ PATTERN NOTES

Yarn weight: DK

Tension: 4.5 x 3tr groups and 9 rows = 10cm (4in)

Striped Cardigan Schematic

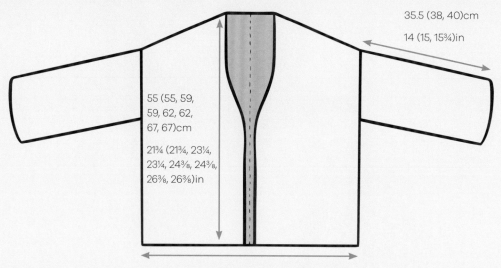

35.5 (38, 40)cm

14 (15, 15¾)in

55 (55, 59, 59, 62, 62, 67, 67)cm

21¾ (21¾, 23¼, 23¼, 24⅜, 24⅜, 26⅜, 26⅜)in

46.5 (51, 57.5, 62, 66.5, 71, 77.5, 82)cm

18¼ (20⅛, 22⅝, 24⅜, 26¼, 28, 30½, 32¼)in

Yardage and Sizing

YARN QUANTITIES:

Please note that for the edge trim, sizes XS, M, 2XL and 4XL use yarn A, and sizes S, L, XL and 3XL use yarn B.

	XS	S	M	L	XL	2XL	3XL	4XL
Yarn A	253g (9oz)/ 708m (774¼yd)	247g (8¾oz)/ 692m (756¾yd)	292g (10⅜oz)/ 818m (894½yd)	287g (10⅛oz)/ 804m (879¼yd)	327g (11½oz)/ 916m (1001¾yd)	371g (13⅛oz)/ 1039m (1136¼yd)	366g (13oz)/ 1025m (1121yd)	411g (14½oz)/ 1151m (1258¾yd)
Yarn B	228g (8oz)/ 638m (698yd)	272g (9⅝oz)/ 762m (833½yd)	267g (9½oz)/ 748m (818yd)	312g (11oz)/ 874m (956yd)	352g (12½oz)/ 986m (1078½yd)	346g (12¼oz)/ 969m (1059¾yd)	391g (13¾oz)/ 1095m (1197½yd)	386g (13⅝oz)/ 1081m (1182¼yd)

SIZING CHART: 17–20CM (6¾–8IN) POSITIVE EASE DEPENDING ON SIZE

	XS	S	M	L	XL	2XL	3XL	4XL
Bust	75cm (29½in)	85cm (33½in)	95cm (37⅜in)	105cm (41⅜in)	115cm (45¼in)	125cm (49¼in)	135cm (53⅛in)	145cm (57⅛in)
Garment circumference	93cm (36⅝in)	102cm (40⅛in)	115cm (45¼in)	124cm (48¾in)	133cm (52⅜in)	142cm (56in)	155cm (61in)	164cm (64½in)
Garment width	46.5cm (18¼in)	51cm (20⅛in)	57.5cm (22⅝in)	62cm (24⅜in)	66.5cm (26¼in)	71cm (28in)	77.5cm (30½in)	82cm (32¼in)
Garment length	55cm (21¾in)	55cm (21¾in)	59cm (23¼in)	59cm (23¼in)	62cm (24⅜in)	62cm (24⅜in)	67cm (26⅜in)	67cm (26⅜in)

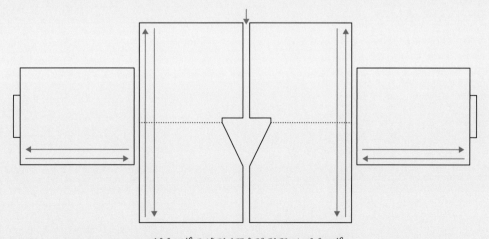

ARROWS INDICATE DIRECTION OF ROWS

Construction

Work front and back panels as one piece, starting from the outer edges and working towards the centre, while increasing on the shoulder line. Extend for the back neck, then join the centre back seam. Reattach yarn and extend for the tapered front panels. Work sleeves vertically, sew up and attach with a seam.

Panel 1

Sizes L, XL, 2XL: Panel 1 will be your right panel.

Sizes XS, S, M, 3XL, 4XL: Panel 1 will be your left panel.

Set up row: Using yarn A, 136 (136, 148, 149, 161, 161, 172, 172) fdc.

Alternatively, 137 (137, 149, 150, 162, 162, 173, 173) ch. 1dc in second ch from hook, 1dc in each ch to end, turn.

On the next row you are going to work groups of 3tr over the dc sts and into the bottom ch.

If you want to you can float your yarns along the end of your work to avoid weaving in lots of ends.

Sizes XS (S, M, 3XL, 4XL) only:

R1 (rs): Attach yarn B to top of first st, 3ch, 1tr into first ch, miss 2 chs, [3tr in next ch, miss 2 chs] 43 (43, 47, 55, 55) times, 3tr in next ch, miss 2ch, 2tr in last ch, turn. 44 (44, 48, 56, 56) 3tr groups.

R2: 3ch, 3tr in next sp, 45 (45, 49, 57, 57) times, 1tr in top of 3ch, turn.

R3: Using yarn A, 3ch, 1tr in same sp, 3tr in next 44 (44, 48, 56, 56) sps, 1tr in last sp, 1tr in top of 3ch, turn.

Size XS only: Work from Shoulder Increases. (Work first row in Yarn A, then continue to work 2 rows in each colour.)

Sizes S (M, 3XL, 4XL) only: R2 and R3 form pattern. Rep pattern 1 (2, 6, 7) more times, changing colour every 2 rows. 5 (7, 15, 17) rows.

Sizes L (XL, 2XL) only:

R1 (rs): Attach yarn B to top of first st, 3ch, miss 1 ch, [3tr in next ch, miss 2 chs] 48 (52, 52) times, 3tr in next ch, miss 1ch, 1tr in last ch, turn. 49 (53, 53) groups.

R2: 3ch, 1tr in same sp, 3tr in next 48 (52, 52) sps, 1tr in last sp, 1tr in top of 3ch, turn.

R3: Using yarn A, 3ch, 3tr in next sp, 49 (53, 53) times, 1tr in top of 3ch, turn.

R2 and R3 form pattern. Rep pattern 2 (4, 5) more times, changing colour every 2 rows. Rep R2 once more. 8 (12, 14 rows).

SHOULDER INCREASES (A)

Continue to change colour every 2 rows to end.

R1: 3ch, *3tr in next 22 (22, 24, 24, 26, 26, 28, 28) sps**, 4tr in next sp, rep from * to **, 1tr in top of 3ch, turn.

R2: 3ch, 1tr in same sp, *3tr in next 22 (22, 24, 24, 26, 26, 28, 28) sps,** 3tr in centre of 4tr group (between second and third tr), rep from * to **, 1tr in last sp, 1tr in top of 3ch, turn.

R3: 3ch, 3tr in next 46 (46, 50, 50, 54, 54, 58, 58) sps, 1tr in top of 3ch, turn.

R4: 3ch, 1tr in same sp, *3tr in next 22 (22, 24, 24, 26, 26, 28, 28) sps,** 4tr in next sp, rep from * to **, in last sp, 1tr in top of 3ch, turn.

R5: 3ch, *3tr in next 23 (23, 25, 25, 27, 27, 29, 29) sps,** 3tr in centre of 4tr group, rep from * to **, 1tr in top of 3ch, turn.

R6: 3ch, 1tr in same sp, 3tr in next 46 (46, 50, 50, 54, 54, 58, 58) sps, 1tr in last sp, 1tr in top of 3ch, turn.

R7: 3ch, *3tr in next 23 (23, 25, 25, 27, 27, 29, 29) sps,** 4tr in next sp, rep from * to **, 1tr in top of 3ch, turn.

R8: 3ch, 1tr in same sp, *3tr in next 23 (23, 25, 25, 27, 27, 29, 29) sps,** 3tr in centre of 4tr group, rep from * to **, 1tr in last sp, 1tr in top of 3ch, turn.

R9: 3ch, 3tr in next 48 (48, 52, 52, 56, 56, 60, 60) sps, 1tr in top of 3ch, turn.

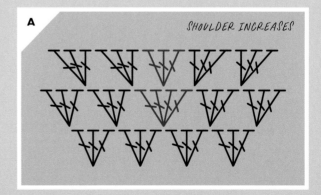

A

SHOULDER INCREASES

R10: 3ch, 1tr in same sp, *3tr in next 23 (23, 25, 25, 27, 27, 29, 29) sps,** 4tr in next sp, rep from *to **, 1tr in last sp, 1tr in top of 3ch, turn.

R11: 3ch, *3tr in next 24 (24, 26, 26, 28, 28, 30, 30) sps,** 3tr in centre of 4tr group, rep from * to **, 1tr in top of 3ch, turn.

R12: 3ch, 1tr in same sp, 3tr in next 48 (48, 52, 52, 56, 56, 60, 60) sps, 1tr in last sp, 1tr in top of 3ch, turn.

R13: 3ch, 3tr in next 49 (49, 53, 53, 57, 57, 61, 61) sps, 1tr in top of 3ch, turn. 16 (18, 20, 21, 25, 27, 28, 30) rows total.

Note: Sizes L, XL and 2XL will finish this section on a single row stripe.

PANEL 1 BACK NECK DECREASE

R1: 3ch, 1tr in same sp, 3tr in next 23 (23, 25, 25, 27, 27, 29, 29) sps, 2tr in next sp, leaving 25 (25, 27, 27, 29, 29, 31, 31) sps unworked, turn.

R2: 3ch, 3tr in next 24 (24, 26, 26, 28, 28, 30, 30) sps, 1tr in top of 3ch, turn.

R3: 3ch, 1tr in same sp, 3tr in next 23 (23, 25, 25, 27, 27, 29, 29) sps, 1tr in last sp, 1tr in top of 3ch, turn.

R2 and R3 form pattern. Rep pattern 2 (2, 2, 2, 2, 2, 3, 3) more times.

Sizes L, XL and 2XL only: Rep R2 once more.

All sizes: Fasten off. Last row will be a single row stripe. 23 (25, 27, 29, 33, 35, 37, 39) rows in total.

Panel 2

Sizes L, XL, 2XL: Panel 2 will be your left panel.

Sizes XS, S, M, 3XL, 4XL: Panel 2 will be your right panel.

Work as for panel 1 to back neck decrease.

PANEL 2 BACK NECK DECREASE

R1: Count 25 (25, 27, 27, 29, 29, 31, 31) sps in from beginning of last row and reattach yarn in sp. 3ch, 1tr in same sp, 3tr in next 23 (23, 25, 25, 27, 27, 29, 29) sps, 1tr in last sp, 1tr in top of 3ch, turn.

Work as R2 from Panel 1 Back Neck Decrease.

Hold the centre back sections together with rs facing each other and sl st together through both loops of each st to form a seam.

PANEL 1 FRONT

Sizes L, XL and 2XL: Use same yarn colour as last row of right panel and change after first row. With ws facing you, count 5 sps down from right neck and attach same colour yarn in sp.

Sizes XS, S, M, 3XL and 4XL: Use next yarn colour and continue to alternate every 2 rows. With rs facing you, count 5 sps down from left neck and attach yarn in sp.

R1: (1ch, 1dc, 1htr, 1tr) in sp, 3tr in next 19 (19, 21, 21, 23, 23, 25, 25) sps, 1tr in next sp, 1tr in top of 3ch, turn.

R2: 3ch, 3tr in next 18 (18, 20, 20, 22, 22, 24, 24) sps, (1tr, 1htr, 1dc) in next sp, turn.

R3: Count 2 sps in and attach yarn or sl st into sp, (1ch, 1dc, 1htr, 1tr) in sp, 3tr in next 16 (16, 18, 18, 20, 20, 22, 22) sps, 1tr in next sp, 1tr in top of 3ch, turn.

R4: 3ch, 3tr in next 15 (15, 17, 17, 19, 19, 21, 21) sps, (1tr, 1htr, 1dc) in next sp, turn.

R5: Count 2 sps in and attach yarn or sl st into sp, (1ch, 1dc, 1htr, 1tr) in sp, 3tr in next 13 (13, 15, 15, 17, 17, 19, 19) sps, 1tr in next sp, 1tr in top of 3ch, turn.

R6: 3ch, 3tr in next 12 (12, 14, 14, 16, 16, 18, 18) sps, (1tr, 1htr, 1dc) in next sp, turn.

Sizes XS, S and M only: End here and fasten off.

R7: Count 2 sps in and attach yarn or sl st into sp, (1ch, 1dc, 1htr, 1tr) in sp, 3tr in next x (x, x, 12, 14, 14, 16, 16) sps, 1tr in next sp, 1tr in top of 3ch, turn.

Sizes L, XL and 2XL only: End here and fasten off.

R8: 3ch, 3tr in next x (x, x, x, x, x, 15, 15) sps, (1tr, 1htr, 1dc) in next sp, fasten off.

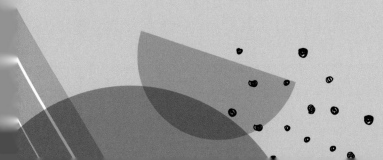

PANEL 2 FRONT

Sizes L, XL and 2XL: Use same yarn colour as last row of left panel and change after first row. Attach yarn to top of last st at left front bottom corner.

Sizes XS, S, M, 3XL and 4XL: Use next yarn colour and continue to alternate every 2 rows. Attach yarn to top of last st at right front bottom corner.

R1: 3ch, 1tr in same sp, 3tr in next 19 (19, 21, 21, 23, 23, 25, 25) sps, (1tr, 1htr, 1dc) in next sp, turn.

R2: Count 2 sps in and attach yarn or sl st into sp, (1ch, 1dc, 1htr, 1tr) in sp, 3tr in next 18 (18, 20, 20, 22, 22, 24, 24) sps, 1tr in top of 3ch, turn.

R3: 3ch, 1tr in same sp, 3tr in next 16 (16, 18, 18, 20, 20, 22, 22) sps, (1tr, 1htr, 1dc) in next sp, turn.

R4: Count 2 sps in and attach yarn or sl st into sp, (1ch, 1dc, 1htr, 1tr) in sp, 3tr in next 15 (15, 17, 17, 19, 19, 21, 21) sps, 1tr in top of 3ch, turn.

R5: 3ch, 1tr in same sp, 3tr in next 13 (13, 15, 15, 17, 17, 19, 19) sps, (1tr, 1htr, 1dc) in next sp, turn.

R6: Count 2 sps in and attach yarn or sl st into sp, (1ch, 1dc, 1htr, 1tr) in sp, 3tr in next 12 (12, 14, 14, 16, 16, 18, 18) sps, 1tr in top of 3ch, turn.

Sizes XS, S and M only: End here and fasten off.

R7: 3ch, 1tr in same sp, 3tr in next x (x, x, 12, 14, 14, 16, 16) sps, (1tr, 1htr, 1dc) in next sp, turn.

Sizes L, XL and 2XL only: End here and fasten off.

R8: Count 2 sps in and attach yarn or sl st into sp, (1ch, 1dc, 1htr, 1tr) in sp, 3tr in next x (x, x, x, x, x, 15, 15) sps, 1tr in top of 3ch, fasten off.

SLEEVES

The sleeve can be made in a choice of three different lengths: S (M, L). S (short) = 35.5cm (14in), M (medium) = 38cm (15in), L (long) = 40cm (15¾in). Follow these size instructions to end of R3. Then work the number of rows required for the garment size you are following for main body.

Set up row: Using yarn A, fdc 50 (53, 56).

Alternatively, 51 (54, 57) ch, turn, 1dc into second ch from hook, 1dc in each ch to end. 50 (53, 56) sts.

In the next row you are going to work groups of 3tr over the dc sts and into the bottom ch.

R1: Using yarn B, 3ch, miss 1 ch, [3tr in next ch, miss 2 chs] 15 (16, 17) times, 3tr in next ch, miss 1 ch, 1tr in last ch, turn. 16 (17, 18) 3tr groups.

R2: 3ch, 1tr in same sp, 3tr in next 15 (16, 17) sps, 1tr in last sp, 1tr in top of 3ch, turn.

R3: Using yarn A, 3ch, 3tr in next 16 (17, 18) sps, 1tr in top of 3ch, turn.

R2 and R3 form pattern. Rep pattern until you have 36 (40, 40, 44, 44, 48, 52, 56) rows, changing colour after every 2 rows. Cut yarn, leaving a long enough tail to sew up the length of the sleeve. Work second sleeve in the same way.

Making Up

Block your panels. With rs facing each other, sew sleeves together along length. Fold front and backs of main body along shoulders (where increases lie) with rs facing each other and ws facing out. Fold sleeve in half lengthways to find the centre of the top edge. Place sleeve with rs facing out inside cardigan. The 3tr groups should be the right way up on the front of the sleeve and upside down on the back of the sleeve. Line up the centre of the top edge of sleeve with the shoulder seam and pin edge of sleeve around edge of main body. Pin down the remaining side seam of the cardigan. Starting at the side seam, sew all around the sleeve, back to the start and down the remaining side seam of the cardigan. Fasten off. Repeat on the other side.

For cuffs and trim, sizes XS, M, 2XL and 4XL use yarn A, sizes S, L, XL and 3XL use yarn B. This is so that the trim contrasts with the last stripe colour on the front panels.

CUFFS

Attach the yarn to the end of the sleeve at the seam and with rs facing, work 2 sl sts per row around sleeve to end. Join to first sl st with a sl st, do not turn. 72 (80, 80, 88, 88, 96, 104, 112) sts.

R1: 4ch, 1dc in second ch from hook, (1ch missed does not count as st), 1dc in each of next 2 chs, sl st across 4 sl sts along edge of sleeve, to anchor your row to the sleeve, turn. 3 sts.

R2: Pull tightly on working yarn to draw cuff together, 1dc in each of the 3sts from R1, turn.

R3: 1ch, 1dc in next 3 sts, sl st across next 4 sl sts along edge of sleeve, turn.

R2 and R3 form pattern. Rep pattern to end. Hold cuff ends with rs facing each other, sl st along the 3 sts to form a seam. Fasten off. Repeat on second sleeve.

EDGING

With rs facing, join yarn at the edge of the back of the neck and work 2 sl sts per row across back of neck to prevent stretching. Fasten off.

Join yarn A at bottom of left front edge and work 2 sl sts per row across hem to bottom of right front edge, turn.

1ch, 1dc in each sl st (under both loops) across hem, back to bottom of left front, turn.

Work back across hem: 1ch, *dc2tog across next 2 sts, 1dc in next st, rep from * to end. If 1 st remains, work 1dc, if 2 sts remain, work dc2tog.

Work around front edges: 1ch, 2dc across side of hem rows, 1dc in each st up right front edge, 1dc in each sl st across back neck, 1dc in each st down left front edge, 2dc across side of hem rows, turn.

Work back around front edges: 1ch, 1dc in each st around to bottom of right front edge, fasten off. Weave in all ends.

Ripple Top

Choose some contrasting colours and hook up this eye-catching cotton top using granny ripple stitch. It has a low back with an elegant tie, so it won't slip off your shoulders while you're dancing.

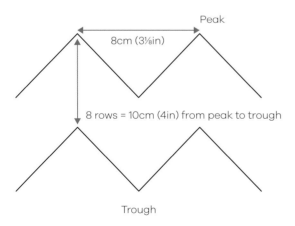

Peak

8cm (3⅛in)

8 rows = 10cm (4in) from peak to trough

Trough

YOU WILL NEED

Hook: 3mm (D), 3.5mm (E/4) for the slip stitches

Scissors

Yarn needle

Yarn: Scheepjes Cotton 8. 100% Cotton, 50g (1¾oz) = 170m (186yd), in the following shades:

- Yarn A: 720 (fuchsia)
- Yarn B: 723 (sea green)
- Yarn C: 722 (ochre)
- Yarn D: 527 (navy)
- Yarn E: 651 (light purple)

PATTERN NOTES

Yarn weight: 4 ply (fingering)

Tension: 6 x 3tr groups and 10 rows = 10cm (4in) over a regular square granny stitch swatch.

To measure your tension (gauge) in ripple stitch pattern, see the diagram to the left. Note that your ripple will be much looser and wider until you have done approx 12 rows so it is advised to measure your panel after 3 stripes to check it matches the width given for your size in the sizing chart, and adjust hook size accordingly.

Ripple Top Schematic

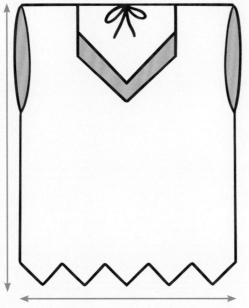

16 (17.5, 19, 20, 21, 22.5, 24, 25)cm

6¼ (6⅞, 7½, 8, 8¼, 8⅞, 9½, 9⅞)in

47.5 (52.5, 52.5, 52.5, 57.5, 57.5, 57.5, 62.5)cm

18¾ (20⅝, 20⅝, 20⅝, 22⅝, 22⅝, 22⅝, 24⅝)in

34.5 (40, 45, 50.5, 53, 58.5, 64, 69)cm

13⅝ (15¾, 17¾, 19⅞, 20⅞, 23, 25¼, 27⅛)in

Yardage and Sizing

YARN QUANTITIES:

	XS	S	M	L	XL	2XL	3XL	4XL
Yarn A	38g (1⅜oz)/ 129m (141⅛yd)	48g (1¾oz)/ 163m (178¼yd)	54g (2oz)/ 184m (201¼yd)	68g (2½oz)/ 231m (252⅝yd)	82g (3oz)/ 279m (305⅛yd)	85g (3oz)/ 289m (316⅛yd)	98g (3½oz)/ 333m (364¼yd)	98g (3½oz)/ 333m (364¼yd)
Yarn B	28g (1oz)/ 95m (104yd)	38g (1⅜oz)/ 129m (141⅛yd)	43g (1½oz)/ 146m (159⅝yd)	48g (1¾oz)/ 163m (178¼yd)	53g (1⅞oz)/ 180m (196⅞yd)	58g (2⅛oz)/ 197m (215½yd)	63g (2¼oz)/ 214m (234yd)	77g (2¾oz)/ 262m (286½yd)
Yarn C	26g (1oz)/ 89m (97¼yd)	34g (1¼oz)/ 116m (126¾yd)	39g (1⅜oz)/ 133m (145½yd)	44g (1½oz)/ 150m (164yd)	51g (1¾oz)/ 174m (190¼yd)	57g (2oz)/ 194m (212¼yd)	62g (2¼oz)/ 211m (230¾yd)	67g (2⅜oz)/ 228m (249½yd)
Yarn D	30g (1⅛oz)/ 102m (111½yd)	32g (1¼oz)/ 109m (119¼yd)	37g (1⅜oz)/ 126m (137¾yd)	42g (1½oz)/ 143m (156⅜yd)	47g (1⅝oz)/ 160m (175yd)	53g (1⅞oz)/ 180m (196⅞yd)	58g (2⅛oz)/ 197m (215½yd)	63g (2¼oz)/ 214m (234yd)
Yarn E	18g (⅝oz)/ 61m (66¾yd)	34g (1¼oz)/ 116m (126¾yd)	38g (1⅜oz)/ 129m (141yd)	41g (1½oz)/ 140m (153⅛yd)	45g (1⅝oz)/ 153m (167⅜yd)	51g (1¾oz)/ 174m (190⅜yd)	56g (2oz)/ 191m (209yd)	61g (2⅛oz)/ 208m (227½yd)

SIZING CHART: 4–8.5CM (1½–3½in) NEGATIVE EASE DEPENDING ON SIZE

	XS	S	M	L	XL	2XL	3XL	4XL
Bust	75cm (29½in)	85cm (33½in)	95cm (37⅜in)	105cm (41⅜in)	115cm (45¼in)	125cm (49¼in)	135cm (53⅛in)	145cm (57⅛in)
Garment circumference	69cm (27⅛in)	80cm (31½in)	90cm (35½in)	101cm (39¾in)	106.5cm (42in)	117cm (46in)	128cm (50⅜in)	138cm (54⅜in)
Garment width	34.5cm (13⅝in)	40cm (15¾in)	45cm (17¾in)	50.5cm (19⅞in)	53cm (20⅞in)	58.5cm (23in)	64cm (25¼in)	69cm (27⅛in)
Garment length	47.5cm (18¾in)	52.5cm (20⅝in)	52.5cm (20⅝in)	52.5cm (20⅝in)	57.5cm (22⅝in)	57.5cm (22⅝in)	57.5cm (22⅝in)	62.5cm (24⅝in)

Construction

Some sizes start and end their rows with a peak/extended peak and some with a trough/extended trough. Pay close attention to the sizing directions for the first four rows. Work in colour order A, B, C, D, E throughout. Change colour every four rows. When fastening off each colour, ensure you leave at least 20cm (8in) of yarn to sew up that section of side seam. To add length, work extra stripes to main body. To bring neckline up one stripe higher, work front panel as for the back panel.

Front

76 (95, 94, 112, 112, 130, 147, 148) ch, using a 3mm (D) hook.

R1 sizes XS (L, XL, 4XL) only: 3tr in fourth ch from hook, miss 2 chs, [(3tr in next ch, miss 2chs) twice, (3tr, 3ch, 3tr) in next ch, (miss 2 chs, 3tr in next ch) twice, miss 5 chs], 3 (5, 5, 7) times, (3tr in next ch, miss 2chs) twice, (3tr, 3ch, 3tr) in next ch, (miss 2 chs, 3tr in next ch) twice, miss 2 chs, 4tr in last ch, turn. 26 (38, 38, 50) groups.

R2 sizes XS (L) only: 3ch, 3tr in each of next 3 sps, [(3tr, 3ch, 3tr) in 3ch sp, 3tr in each of next 2 sps, miss next sp, 3tr in each of next 2 sps] 3 (5) times, (3tr, 3ch, 3tr) in 3ch sp, 3tr in each of next 3 sps, 1tr in sp between third tr and 3ch of last group, turn.

R3 sizes XS (L) only: Work as R2 but work last 1tr in top of 3ch, turn.

R2 sizes XL (4XL) only: 3ch, 3tr in sp between first and second tr in group, 3tr in each of next 3 sps, [(3tr, 3ch, 3tr) in 3ch sp, 3tr in each of next 2 sps, miss next sp, 3tr in each of next 2 sps] 5 (7) times, (3tr, 3ch, 3tr) in 3ch sp, 3tr in each of next 3 sps, 4tr in sp between third tr and 3ch of last group, turn. 40 (52) groups.

R3 sizes XL (4XL) only: 3ch, 3tr in each of next 4 sps, [(3tr, 3ch, 3tr) in 3ch sp, 3tr in each of next 2 sps, miss next sp, 3tr in each of next 2 sps] 5 (7) times, (3tr, 3ch, 3tr) in 3ch sp, 3tr in each of next 4 sps, 1tr in sp between third tr and 3ch of last group, turn.

R4 sizes XL (4XL) only: Work as R3 but work last 1tr in top of 3ch, turn.

R1 size S only: 3tr in 5th ch from hook, [(miss 2 chs, 3tr in next ch) twice, miss 5 chs, (3tr in next ch, miss 2 chs) twice, (3tr, 3ch, 3tr) in next ch] 4 times, miss 2 chs, 3tr in next ch) twice, miss 5 chs, (3tr in next ch, miss 2 chs) twice, (3tr, 1ch, 1tr) in last ch, turn. 30 groups.

R2 size S only: (4ch, 3tr) in 1ch sp, [3tr in each of next 2 sps, miss next sp, 3tr in each of next 2 sps, (3tr, 3ch, 3tr) in 3ch sp] 4 times, 3tr in each of next 2 sps, miss next sp, 3tr in each of next 2 sps, (3tr, 1ch, 1tr) in 4ch sp, turn.

R1 sizes M and 2XL only: (3tr, 3ch, 3tr) in fourth ch from hook, [(miss 2 chs, 3tr in next ch) twice, miss 5 chs, (3tr in next ch, miss 2 chs) twice, (3tr, 3ch, 3tr) in next ch] 5 (7) times, work 1tr more in last ch to form a 4tr group, turn. 32 (44) groups.

R2 size M only: (3ch, 3tr) in sp between first and second tr in group, [(3tr, 3ch, 3tr) in 3ch sp, 3tr in each of next 2 sps, miss next sp, 3tr in each of next 2 sps] 5 times, (3tr, 3ch, 3tr) in 3ch sp, 4tr in sp between third tr and 3ch of last group, turn. 34 groups.

R3 size M only: 3ch, 3tr in next sp, [(3tr, 3ch, 3tr) in 3ch sp, 3tr in each of next 2 sps, miss next sp, 3tr in each of next 2 sps] 5 times, (3tr, 3ch, 3tr) in 3ch sp, 3tr in next sp, 1tr in sp between third tr and 3ch of last group, turn.

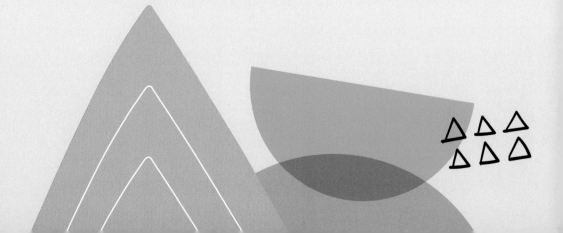

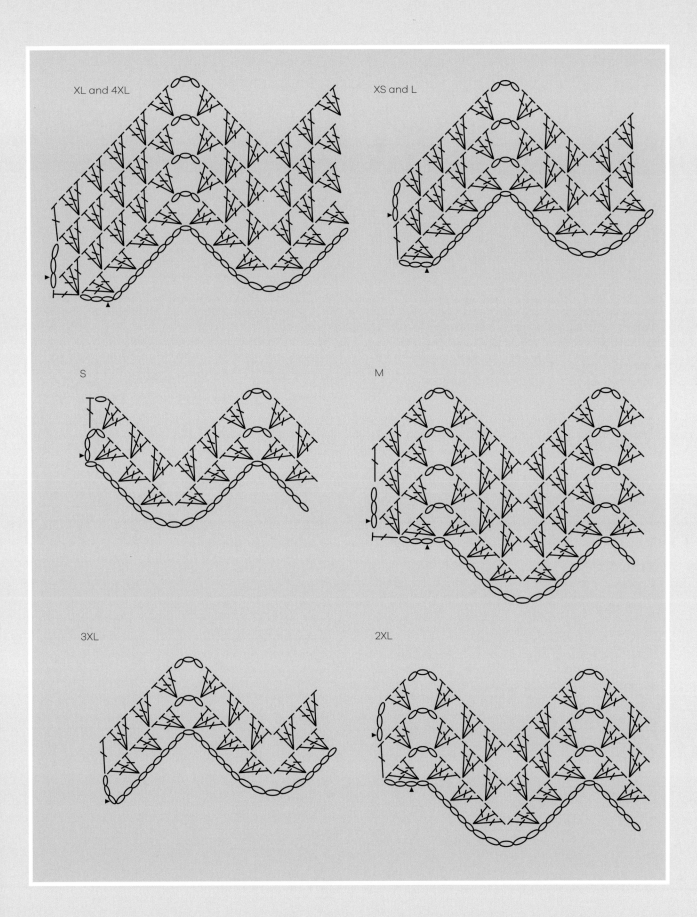

XL and 4XL

XS and L

S

M

3XL

2XL

R4 size M only: Work as R3 but work last 1tr in top of 3ch, turn.

R2 size 2XL only: 3ch, [(3tr, 3ch, 3tr) in 3ch sp, 3tr in each of next 2 sps, miss next sp, 3tr in each of next 2 sps] 7 times, (3tr, 3ch, 3tr) in 3ch sp, 1tr in sp between third tr and 3ch of last group, turn.

R3 size 2XL only: Work as R2 but work last 1tr in top of 3ch, turn.

R1 size 3XL only: 3tr in 6th ch from hook, [miss 2 chs, 3tr in next ch, miss 2 chs, (3tr, 3ch, 3tr) in next ch, (miss 2 chs, 3tr in next ch) twice, miss 5 chs, 3tr in next ch], 7 times, miss 2 chs, 3tr in next ch, miss 2 chs, (3tr, 3ch, 3tr) in next ch, (miss 2 chs, 3tr in next ch) twice, miss 2chs, 1tr in last ch, turn. 48 groups.

R2 size 3XL only: 3ch, 3tr in each of next 2 sps, [(3tr, 3ch, 3tr) in 3ch sp, 3tr in each of next 2 sps, miss next sp, 3tr in each of next 2 sps] 7 times, (3tr, 3ch, 3tr) in 3ch sp, 3tr in each of next 2 sps, 1tr in top of 3ch, turn.

All sizes: Rep R3 (R2, R4, R3, R4, R3, R2, R4) until you have 20 (24, 24, 24, 28, 28, 28, 32) rows, changing colour every 4 rows. 5 (6, 6, 6, 7, 7, 7, 8) stripes.

LEFT FRONT NECKLINE SHAPING

Begin all odd rows and end all even rows in the same stitch pattern as R3 (R2, R4, R3, R4, R3, R2, R4) and work instructions as given below for shaping the neckline.

Locate the central trough in your last ripple stripe (A).

R1: With rs facing, using next colour, follow stitch pattern to the last peak before the central trough (B) 3tr in 3ch sp at peak, turn. 10 (12, 14, 16, 17, 19, 21, 23) groups (B).

R2: 3ch, 3tr in next 2 sps, miss next sp and follow stitch pattern to end of row, turn. 9 (11, 13, 15, 16, 18, 20, 22) groups.

R3: Follow stitch pattern to the sp between 3tr and 3ch, 3tr in sp, turn.

R4: 3ch, 3tr in next sp, miss next sp and follow stitch pattern to end of row, turn. 8 (10, 12, 14, 15, 17, 19, 21) groups.

R5: Using next colour, follow stitch pattern to sp between 3tr and 3ch, 3tr in sp, turn.

R6: 3ch, miss next sp, 3tr in next 3 sps, follow stitch pattern to end of row, turn. 7 (9, 11, 13, 14, 16, 18, 20) groups.

R7: Follow stitch pattern to last peak, (3tr, 3ch, 3tr) in 3ch sp, 3tr in next sp, 1tr in next sp, turn. 6 (8, 10, 12, 13, 15, 17, 19) groups.

R8: 3ch, 3tr in next sp, (3tr, 3ch, 3tr) in 3ch sp, follow stitch pattern to end of row, turn.

R9–R12: Using next colour, rep (R7, R8) twice. 32 (36, 36, 36, 40, 40, 40, 44) rows.

STRAIGHTEN LEFT FRONT TOP EDGE

OUTER CORNER:

Using next colour, with rs facing, join yarn to last sp of last row.

Note: Size S has no outer corner – work from troughs section (B).

Size 2XL only: Miss R1–R5a, work R5b, miss R6, then sl st into third ch of 3ch sp.

R1: 3ch, 3tr in next 3 (x, 1, 3, 4, x, 2, 4) sps, 1tr in 3ch sp, turn.

Size M only: Go to R5a.

R2: 3ch, 3tr in next 2 (x, x, 2, 3, x, 1, 3) sps, 1tr in last sp, turn.

Size 3XL only: Go to R5b.

R3: 3ch, 3tr in next 1 (x, x, 1, 2, x, x, 2) sps, 1tr in last sp, turn.

Sizes XS and L only: Go to R5a.

R4: Sizes XL and 4XL only - 3ch, 3tr in next sp, 1tr in last sp, turn. Go to R5b.

R5a: 1dc in top of first tr, 1dc in top of second tr, 1htr in top of third tr, 1tr in top of 3ch, turn.

R5b: 3ch, 1htr in top of first tr, 1dc in top of second tr, 1dc in top of third tr.

R6: Sl st along the top edge back into 3ch sp, sl st into third ch of 3ch sp.

Size XS only: Miss troughs section and work from inner corner.

TROUGHS ALL SIZES:

R1: 3ch, 3tr in next 2 sps, miss next sp, 3tr in next 2 sps, 1tr in 3ch sp, turn.

R2: 3ch, 3tr in next sp, miss next sp, 3tr in next sp, 1tr in last sp, turn.

R3: 1dc in top of first tr, 1dc in top of second tr, 1htr in top of third tr, 1htr in top of first tr in next group, 1dc in top of second tr, 1dc in top of third tr. Sl st along the side of 3ch and 1tr, sl st into 3ch sp, sl st in third ch of 3ch sp.

Sizes 2XL–4XL only: In second trough, rep R1–R3 once more.

INNER CORNER:

R1: 3ch, 3tr in next sp, 1tr in last sp, turn.

R2: 3ch, 1htr in top of first tr, 1dc in top of second tr, 1dc in top of third tr, fasten off.

RIGHT FRONT NECKLINE SHAPING

When joining on a new colour at the neckline edge, leave a 25cm (9⅞in) yarn tail for slip stitching around that section of neckline.

R1: With rs facing, using next colour, join yarn to the next peak on the opposite side of the central trough, 3ch, 2tr in 3ch sp at peak, follow stitch pattern to end of row, turn. 10 (12, 14, 16, 17, 19, 21, 23) groups.

R2: Follow stitch pattern to last sp, 3tr in last sp, 1tr in top of last tr in group, turn. 9 (11, 13, 15, 16, 18, 20, 22) groups.

R3: 3ch, 2tr in sp between 1tr and 3tr, follow stitch pattern to end of row, turn.

R4: Rep R2. 8 (10, 12, 14, 15, 17, 19, 21) groups.

R5: Using next colour, 3ch, 2tr in sp between 1tr and 3tr, miss next sp, 3tr in next sp, follow stitch pattern to end of row, turn.

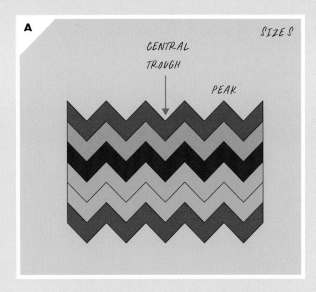

A   SIZES S

CENTRAL TROUGH

PEAK

B   SIZES S

LEFT SHOULDER STRAIGHTENING SECTION. SIZE M

INNER CORNER
(Nearest to neck)

TROUGH

OUTER CORNER
(Nearest to shoulder)

R6: Follow stitch pattern to sp before last sp, 3tr in sp, miss next sp, 1tr in top of last tr in group, turn. 7 (9, 11, 13, 14, 16, 18, 20) groups.

R7: Sl st back across top of first 3tr group, sl st into next sp, 3ch, 3tr in next sp, (3tr, 3ch, 3tr) in 3ch sp, follow stitch pattern to end of row, turn. 6 (8, 10, 12, 13, 15, 17, 19) groups.

R8: Follow stitch pattern to sp before last sp, 3tr in sp, 1tr in last sp, turn.

R9: Using next colour, 3ch, 3tr in next sp, (3tr, 3ch, 3tr) in 3ch sp, follow stitch pattern to end of row, turn.

R10: Follow stitch pattern to last peak, (3tr, 3ch, 3tr) in 3ch sp, 3tr in next sp, 1tr in top of 3ch, turn.

R11: Rep R9 in same colour.

R12: Rep R10.

STRAIGHTEN RIGHT FRONT TOP EDGE

INNER CORNER:

Using next colour, with rs facing, join yarn to last sp of last row on neckline edge.

R1: 3ch, 3tr in next sp, 1tr in 3ch sp, turn.

R2: 1dc in first tr of group, 1dc in second tr of group, 1htr in third tr of group, 1tr in top of 3ch, turn.

Sl st along all the sts back to 3ch sp, sl st in third ch of 3ch sp.

TROUGHS:

Work as troughs section for Straighten Left Front Top Edge (XS has no trough - move to outer corner).

OUTER CORNER:

Size S has no outer corner: Fasten off after troughs section.

Size 2XL only: Miss R1–R5a, work R5b.

R1: 3ch, 3tr in next 3 (x, 1, 3, 4, x, 2, 4) sps, 1tr in last sp, turn.

Size M only: Go to R5a.

R2: 3ch, 3tr in next 2 (x, x, 2, 3, x, 1, 3) sps, 1tr in last sp, turn.

Size 3XL only: Go to R5b.

R3: 3ch, 3tr in next 1 (x, x, 1, 2, x, x, 2) sps, 1tr in last sp, turn.

Sizes XS and L only: Go to R5a.

R4, sizes XL and 4XL only: 3ch, 3tr in next sp, 1tr in last sp, turn. Go to R5b.

R5a: 3ch, 1htr in top of first tr, 1dc in top of second tr, 1dc in top of third tr, fasten off.

R5b: 1dc in top of first tr, 1dc in top of second tr, 1htr in top of third tr, 1tr in top of 3ch, fasten off.

Back

Work as for the front until you have 24 (28, 28, 28, 32, 32, 32, 36) rows, changing colour every 4 rows. 6 (7, 7, 7, 8, 8, 8, 9) stripes.

RIGHT BACK NECKLINE SHAPING

Work as Left Front Neckline Shaping to R8. Miss R9–R12 and work straightening sections.

LEFT BACK NECKLINE SHAPING

Work as Right Front Neckline Shaping to R8. Miss R9–R12 and work straightening sections.

FINISHING

Block your panels, then with rs facing each other, sew front to back at shoulder seams in matching colour yarn. Sew up side seams leaving last 11 (12, 13, 14, 15, 16, 17, 18) rows (not including straightening rows), open for armholes.

Optional: With rs facing each other, join matching yarn to inner edge of shoulder seam, using a 3.5mm (E/4) hook, sl st evenly all around neckline, working (5 sl sts across every 2 rows), changing colour to match each stripe. Sl st to first sl st at end, fasten off. This will prevent the neckline stretching. Repeat around both armholes.

Ties

Attach matching yarn to inner edge of shoulder seam, using a 3mm (D) hook, 70ch. Using a 3.5mm (E/4) hook, 1 sl st in second ch and in each ch to end, sl st to shoulder seam, fasten off. Repeat on opposite shoulder seam. Tie in a loose bow at back.

With rs facing attach yarn A to the bottom of side seam. 1ch, 1dc in each ch around the hem, working 3dc in the third ch of each 5ch sp to form a point. Sl st to top of first dc, fasten off.

Weave in ends.

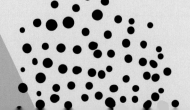

V-neck Jumper

This slouchy, seamless jumper is made in a lightweight DK yarn, giving it plenty of drape. It's great for snuggling in on those lazy winter days, and can be worn on or off the shoulder, tucked in or loose, making it super versatile.

◇ YOU WILL NEED

Hook: 4mm (G/6)

Scissors

Yarn needle

4 x stitch markers

Yarn: Drops Sky. 74% Alpaca, 18% Polyamide, 8% Wool, 50g (1¾oz) = 190m (208yd)

Shade: Curry (17)

◇ PATTERN NOTES

Yarn weight: DK

Tension: 5 x 3tr groups and 11 rows = 10cm (4in)

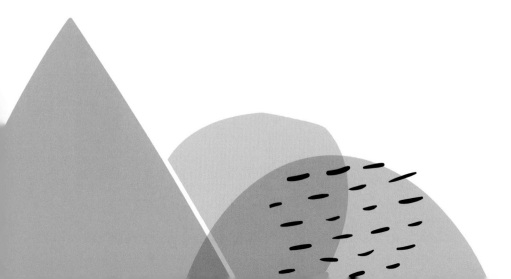

V-neck Schematic

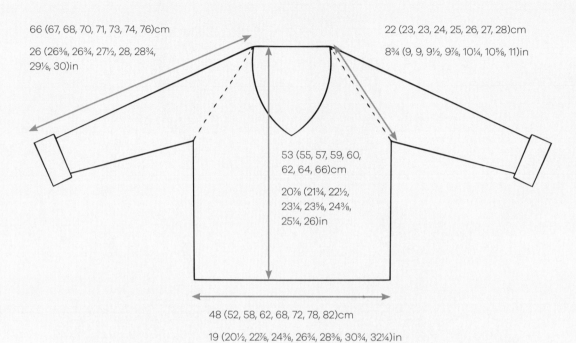

66 (67, 68, 70, 71, 73, 74, 76)cm

26 (26⅜, 26¾, 27½, 28, 28¾, 29⅛, 30)in

22 (23, 23, 24, 25, 26, 27, 28)cm

8¾ (9, 9, 9½, 9⅞, 10¼, 10⅝, 11)in

53 (55, 57, 59, 60, 62, 64, 66)cm

20⅞ (21¾, 22½, 23¼, 23⅝, 24⅜, 25¼, 26)in

48 (52, 58, 62, 68, 72, 78, 82)cm

19 (20½, 22⅞, 24⅜, 26¾, 28⅜, 30¾, 32¼)in

Yardage and Sizing

YARN QUANTITIES:

XS	S	M	L	XL	2XL	3XL	4XL
425g (15oz)/ 1615m (1766¼yd)	460g (16¼oz)/ 1748m (1911⅝yd)	500g (17¾oz)/ 1900m (2078yd)	543g (19¼oz)/ 2063m (2256¼yd)	598g (21⅛oz)/ 2272m (2484¾yd)	639g (22½oz)/ 2428m (2655⅜yd)	698g (24¾oz)/ 2652m (2900¼yd)	739g (26⅛oz)/ 2808m (3071yd)

SIZING CHART: 19-21CM (7½–8¼IN) POSITIVE EASE DEPENDING ON SIZE

	XS	S	M	L	XL	2XL	3XL	4XL
Bust	75cm (29½in)	85cm (33½in)	95cm (37⅜in)	105cm (41⅜in)	115cm (45¼in)	125cm (49¼in)	135cm (53⅛in)	145cm (57⅛in)
Garment circumference	96cm (37¾in)	104cm (41in)	116cm (45¾in)	124cm (48¾in)	136cm (53½in)	144cm (56¾in)	156cm (61½in)	164cm (64½in)
Garment width	48cm (19in)	52cm (20½in)	58cm (22⅞in)	62cm (24⅜in)	68cm (26¾in)	72cm (28⅜in)	78cm (30¾in)	82cm (32¼in)
Garment length	53cm (20⅞in)	55cm (21¾in)	57cm (22½in)	59cm (23¼in)	60cm (23⅝in)	62cm (24⅜in)	64cm (25¼in)	66cm (26in)
Sleeve length from neck	66cm (26in)	67cm (26⅜in)	68cm (26¾in)	70cm (27½in)	71cm (28in)	73cm (28¾in)	74cm (29⅛in)	76cm (30in)

Construction

This jumper is worked from the top down in a raglan style. The body and sleeves are worked seamlessly onto the yoke. The sleeve turn ups are optional and the body and sleeve length can be customized easily.

Body

Set up round: 34 (37, 40, 40, 49, 49, 52, 52) fdc.

Alternatively, 35 (38, 41, 41, 50, 50, 53, 53) ch. 1dc in second ch from hook, 1dc in each ch to end. 34 (37, 40, 40, 49, 49, 52, 52) sts.

On the next row you are going to work groups of 3tr over the dc sts and into the bottom ch.

R1: 3ch, 1tr in same ch, *(miss 2 chs, 3tr in next ch) 1 (1, 1, 1, 2, 2, 2, 2) times, miss 2 chs, 2tr in next ch,** (miss 2 chs, 3tr in next ch) 6 (7, 8, 8, 9, 9, 10, 10) times, miss 2 chs, 2tr in next ch, rep from * to **, the last 2tr should be in the last ch, turn.

Note: 2tr in r-sp means work 2tr into the raglan sp, which is the sp between the 2 sts of the 2tr group in the prev row. At the end of this row, place a st marker in each of your 4 raglan sps, and continue to move markers up into your new raglan groups as you work so that you do not accidentally work past them, or confuse them with other 2tr groups that will appear later on (A).

R2: 3ch, 2tr in r-sp, *3tr in each of next 2 (2, 2, 2, 3, 3, 3, 3) sps, 2tr in r-sp, ** 3tr in each of next 7 (8, 9, 9, 10, 10, 11, 11) sps, 2tr in r-sp, rep from * to ** 1tr in top of 3ch, turn.

R3: 3ch, 2tr in top of last st, 2tr in r-sp, *3tr in each of next 3 (3, 3, 3, 4, 4, 4, 4) sps, 2tr in r-sp, ** 3tr in each of next 8 (9, 10, 10, 11, 11, 12, 12) sps, 2tr in r-sp, rep from * to ** 3tr in top of 3ch, turn.

You will have 1 3tr group across each front, 3 (3, 3, 3, 4, 4, 4, 4) 3tr groups across each shoulder and 8 (9, 10, 10, 11, 11, 12, 12) 3tr groups across the back, in addition to your 4 raglan (2tr) groups.

Over the next 3 rows you will work decreases on either side of your raglan groups to prevent the yoke from increasing too quickly (B).

R4: 3ch, 1tr in top of same st, 2tr in sp between 3tr group and raglan group, 2tr in r-sp, *2tr in next sp, 3tr in each of next 2 (2, 2, 2, 3, 3, 3, 3) sps, 2tr in last sp, 2tr in r-sp,** 2tr in next sp, 3tr in each of next 7 (8, 9, 9, 10, 10, 11, 11) sps, 2tr in next sp, 2tr in r-sp, rep from * to **, 2tr in next sp, 2tr in top of 3ch, turn.

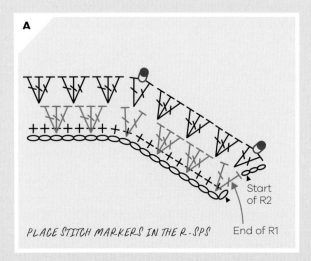

PLACE STITCH MARKERS IN THE R-SPS

Start of R2

End of R1

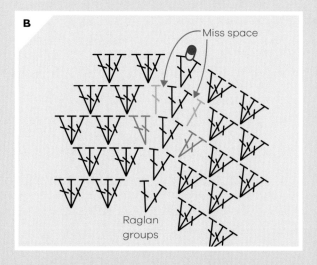

Miss space

Raglan groups

R5: 3ch, 3tr in sp between 2tr groups, 1tr in last sp, 2tr in r-sp, *1tr in next sp, 3tr in each of next 3 (3, 3, 3, 4, 4, 4, 4) sps, 1tr in last sp, 2tr in r-sp,** 1tr in next sp, 3tr in each of next 8 (9, 10, 10, 11, 11, 12, 12) sps, 1tr in next sp, 2tr in r-sp, rep from * to **, 1tr in next sp, 3tr in next sp, 1tr in top of 3ch, turn.

R6: 3ch, 2tr in top of same st, 3tr in next sp, miss next sp, 2tr in r-sp, *miss next sp, 3tr in each of next 4 (4, 4, 4, 5, 5, 5, 5) sps, miss last sp, 2tr in r-sp,** miss next sp, 3tr in each of next 9 (10, 11, 11, 12, 12, 13, 13) sps, miss next sp, 2tr in r-sp, rep from * to **, miss next sp, 3tr in next sp, 3tr in top of 3ch, turn.

R7: 3ch, 1tr in top of same st, 3tr in each of next 2 sps, 2tr in r-sp, *3tr in each of next 5 (5, 5, 5, 6, 6, 6, 6) sps, 2tr in r-sp, ** 3tr in each of next 10 (11, 12, 12, 13, 13, 14, 14) sps, 2tr in r-sp, rep from * to **, 3tr in each of next 2 sps, 2tr in top of 3ch, turn.

R8: 3ch, 3tr in each of next 3 sps, 2tr in r-sp, *3tr in each of next 6 (6, 6, 6, 7, 7, 7, 7) sps, 2tr in r-sp,** 3tr in each of next 11 (12, 13, 13, 14, 14, 15, 15) sps, 2tr in r-sp, rep from * to **, 3tr in each of next 3 sps, 1tr in top of 3ch, turn.

R9: 3ch, 2tr in same sp, 3tr in each of next 3 sps, 2tr in r-sp, *3tr in each of next 7 (7, 7, 7, 8, 8, 8, 8) sps, 2tr in r-sp,** 3tr in each of next 12 (13, 14, 14, 15, 15, 16, 16) sps, 2tr in r-sp, rep from * to **, 3tr in each of next 3 sps, 3tr in top of 3ch, turn.

R10: 3ch, 1tr in same sp, 3tr in each of next 3 sps, 2tr in next sp, 2tr in r-sp, *2tr in next sp, 3tr in each of next 6 (6, 6, 6, 7, 7, 7, 7) sps, 2tr in next sp, 2tr in r-sp,** 2tr in next sp, 3tr in each of next 11 (12, 13, 13, 14, 14, 15, 15) sps, 2tr in next sp, 2tr in r-sp, rep from * to **, 2tr in next sp, 3tr in each of next 3 sps, 2tr in top of 3ch, turn.

R11: 3ch, 3tr in each of next 4 sps, 1tr in next sp, 2tr in r-sp, *1tr in next sp, 3tr in each of next 7 (7, 7, 7, 8, 8, 8, 8) sps, 1tr in next sp, 2tr in r-sp,** 1tr in next sp, 3tr in each of next 12 (13, 14, 14, 15, 15, 16, 16) sps, 1tr in next sp, 2tr in r-sp, rep from * to **, 1tr in next sp, 3tr in each of next 4 sps, 1tr in top of 3ch, turn.

R12: 3ch, 2tr in same sp, 3tr in each of next 4 sps, miss next sp, 2tr in r-sp, *miss next sp, 3tr in each of next 8 (8, 8, 8, 9, 9, 9, 9) sps, miss next sp, 2tr in r-sp,** miss next sp, 3tr in each of next 13 (14, 15, 15, 16, 16, 17, 17) sps, miss next sp, 2tr in r-sp, rep from * to **, miss next sp, 3tr in each of next 4 sps, 3tr in top of 3ch, turn.

R13: 3ch, 1tr in same sp, 3tr in each of next 5 sps, 2tr in r-sp, *3tr in each of next 9 (9, 9, 9, 10, 10, 10, 10) sps, 2tr in r-sp, ** 3tr in each of next 14 (15, 16, 16, 17, 17, 18, 18) sps, 2tr in r-sp, rep from * to **, 3tr in each of next 5 sps, 2tr in top of 3ch, turn.

R14: 3ch, 3tr in each of next 6 sps, 2tr in r-sp, *3tr in each of next 10 (10, 10, 10, 11, 11, 11, 11) sps, 2tr in r-sp, ** 3tr in each of next 15 (16, 17, 17, 18, 18, 19, 19) sps, 2tr in r-sp, rep from * to **, 3tr in each of next 6 sps, 1tr in top of 3ch, turn.

R15: 3ch, 2tr in same sp, 3tr in each of next 6 sps, 2tr in r-sp, *3tr in each of next 11 (11, 11, 11, 12, 12, 12, 12) sps, 2tr in r-sp,** 3tr in each of next 16 (17, 18, 18, 19, 19, 20, 20) sps, 2tr in r-sp, rep from * to **, 3tr in each of next 6 sps, 3tr in top of 3ch, turn.

R16: 3ch, 1tr in top of same st, 3tr in each of next 6 sps, 2tr in next sp, 2tr in r-sp, *3 (3, 2, 2, 2, 2, 2, 2) tr in next sp, 3tr in each of next 10 (10, 10, 10, 11, 11, 11, 11) sps, 3 (3, 2, 2, 2, 2, 2, 2) tr in next sp, 2tr in r-sp**, 2tr in next sp, 3tr in each of next 15 (16, 17, 17, 18, 18, 19, 19) sps, 2tr in next sp, 2tr in r-sp, rep from * to **, 2tr in next sp, 3tr in next 6 sps, 2tr in top of 3ch, turn.

R17: 3ch, 3tr in each of next 7 sps, 1tr in next sp, 2tr in r-sp, *3 (3, 1, 1, 1, 1, 1, 1) tr in next sp, 3tr in each of next 11 (11, 11, 11, 12, 12, 12, 12) sps, 3 (3, 1, 1, 1, 1, 1, 1) tr in next sp, 2tr in r-sp**, 1tr in next sp, 3tr in each of next 16 (17, 18, 18, 19, 19, 20, 20) sps, 1tr in next sp, 2tr in r-sp, rep from * to **, 1tr in next sp, 3tr in next 7 sps, 1tr in top of 3ch, turn.

R18: 3ch, 2tr in top of same st, 3tr in each of next 7 sps, miss next sp, 2tr in r-sp *(sizes M–4XL only: miss next sp) 3tr in each of next 14 (14, 12, 12, 13, 13, 13, 13) sps (sizes M–4XL only: miss next sp) 2tr in r-sp**, miss next sp, 3tr in each of next 17 (18, 19, 19, 20, 20, 21, 21) sps, miss next sp, 2tr in r-sp, rep from * to **, miss next sp, 3tr in next 7 sps, 3tr in top of 3ch, turn.

R19: 3ch, 2 (2, 2, 2, 2, 2, 1, 1) tr in same sp, 3tr in each of next 8 sps, 2tr in r-sp, *3tr in each of next 15 (15, 13, 13, 14, 14, 14, 14) sps, 2tr in r-sp, ** 3tr in each of next 18 (19, 20, 20, 21, 21, 22, 22) sps, 2tr in r-sp, rep from * to ** 3tr in each of next 8 sps, 3 (3, 3, 3, 3, 3, 2, 2) tr in top of 3ch turn.

Size XS only: At end of R19, 1ch and join to top of 3ch with a sl st to join fronts together, fasten off. Work from Joined Yoke R1 (A).

R20: 3ch, x (2, 2, 2, 2, 2, 0, 0) tr in same sp, 3tr in each of next 9 sps, 2tr in r-sp, *3tr in each of next x (16, 14, 14, 15, 15, 15, 15) sps, 2tr in r-sp, ** 3tr in each of next x (20, 21, 21, 22, 22, 23, 23) sps, 2tr in r-sp, rep from * to ** 3tr in each of next 9 sps, x (3, 3, 3, 3, 3, 1, 1) tr in top of 3ch turn.

Size S only: At end of R20, 1ch and join to top of 3ch with a sl st to join fronts together, fasten off. Work from Joined Yoke R1.

R21: 3ch, 2tr in same st, 3tr in each of next x (x, 10, 10, 10, 10, 9, 9) sps, 2tr in r-sp, *3tr in each of next x (x, 15, 15, 16, 16, 16, 16) sps, 2tr in r-sp**, 3tr in each of next x (x, 22, 22, 23, 23, 24, 24) sps, 2tr in r-sp, rep from * to **, 3tr in each of next x (x, 10, 10, 10, 10, 9, 9) sps, 3tr in top of 3ch, turn.

Sizes M and L only: At end of R21, 1ch and join to top of 3ch with a sl st to join fronts together, fasten off. Work from Joined Yoke R1.

R22: 3ch, 2tr in same st, 3tr in each of next x (x, x, x, 10, 10, 9, 9) sps, x (x, x, x, 2, 2, 3, 3) tr in next sp, 2tr in r-sp, *2tr in next sp, 3tr in each of next 15 sps, 2tr in next sp, 2tr in r-sp,** 2tr in next sp, 3tr in each of next x (x, x, x, 22, 22, 23, 23) sps, 2tr in next sp, 2tr in r-sp, rep from * to ** x (x, x, x, 2, 2, 3, 3) tr in next sp, 3tr in each of next x (x, x, x, 10, 10, 9, 9) sps, 3tr in top of 3ch, turn.

Sizes XL and 2XL only: At end of R22, 1ch and join to top of 3ch with a sl st to join fronts together, fasten off. Work from Joined Yoke R1.

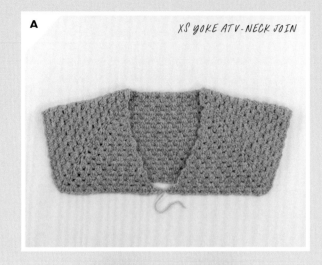

A

XS YOKE AT V-NECK JOIN

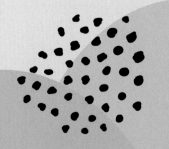

R23: 3ch, 2tr in same st, 3tr in each of next 11 sps, 2tr in r-sp, * 1tr in next sp, 3tr in each of next 16 sps, 1tr in next sp, 2tr in r-sp,** 1tr in next sp, 3tr in each of next 24 sps, 1tr in next sp, 2tr in r-sp, rep from * to ** 3tr in each of next 11 sps, 3tr in top of 3ch, 1ch, join to top of 3ch with a sl st to join fronts together, fasten off. Work from Joined Yoke R1.

JOINED YOKE R1

With the ws of the stitches in the previous row facing you, count 10 (11, 12, 12, 13, 13, 13, 13) sps in from right back raglan group (as facing you) to the centre of the back and attach yarn in sp.

Note: When the number of trebles given is 0, miss this sp. Back and front will have same st count from this point.

Back: 3ch, 2tr in same sp, 3tr in each of next 8 (9, 10, 10, 11, 11, 12, 12) sps, 3 (3, 2, 2, 1, 1, 0, 0) tr in next sp, 2tr in r-sp,

Sleeve: *3 (3, 3, 3, 1, 1, 0, 0) tr in next sp, 3tr in each of next 14 (15, 14, 14, 16, 16, 17, 17) sps, 3 (3, 3, 3, 1, 1, 0, 0) tr in next sp, 2tr in r-sp,**

Front: 3 (3, 2, 2, 1, 1, 3, 3) tr in next sp, 3tr in each of the next 8 (9, 10, 10, 11, 11, 11, 11) sps, 3tr in 1ch at front join, 3tr in each of the next 8 (9, 10, 10, 11, 11, 11, 11) sps, 3 (3, 2, 2, 1, 1, 3, 3) tr in next sp, 2tr in r-sp,

Rep from * to ** for second sleeve.

Back: 3 (3, 2, 2, 1, 1, 0, 0) tr in next sp, 3tr in remaining 8 (9, 10, 10, 11, 11, 12, 12) sps to end, join to top of 3ch with a sl st, turn.

JOINED YOKE R2

Note: When the number of trebles given is 0, miss this sp.

Back: 3ch, 2tr in same sp, 3tr in each sp to sp before r-sp, 3 (2, 1, 1, 0, 0, 3, 3) tr in sp, 2tr in r-sp,

Sleeve: *3 (3, 3, 3, 0, 0, 3, 3) tr in next sp, 3tr in each of next 15 (16, 15, 15, 17, 17, 16, 16) sps, 3 (3, 3, 3, 0, 0, 3, 3) tr in next sp, 2tr in r-sp,**

Front: 3 (2, 1, 1, 0, 0, 3, 3) tr in next sp, 3tr in each of next 18 (20, 22, 22, 24, 24, 24, 24) sps, 3 (2, 1, 1, 0, 0, 3, 3) tr in sp before r-sp, 2tr in r-sp,

Rep from * to ** for second sleeve.

Back: 3 (2, 1, 1, 0, 0, 3, 3) tr in next sp, 3tr in each sp to end, join to top of 3ch with a sl st, turn.

TIP

CHECK YOUR ROW TENSION (GAUGE) FREQUENTLY TO ENSURE THAT YOUR NECKLINE AND UNDERARMS DO NOT END UP TOO DEEP.

JOINED YOKE R3

Note: When the number of trebles given is 0, miss this sp.

Back: 3ch, 2tr in same sp, 3tr in each sp to sp before r-sp, 2 (1, 0, 0, 3, 3, 3, 3) tr in sp, 2tr in r-sp,

Sleeve: *3tr in each of next 18 (19, 18, 18, 18, 18, 19, 19) sps, 2tr in r-sp,**

Front: 2 (1, 0, 0, 3, 3, 3, 3) tr in next sp, 3tr in each of next 19 (21, 23, 23, 23, 23, 25, 25) sps, 2 (1, 0, 0, 3, 3, 3, 3) tr in sp before r-sp, 2tr in r-sp,

Rep from * to ** for second sleeve.

Back: 2 (1, 0, 0, 3, 3, 3, 3) tr in next sp, 3tr in each sp to end, join to top of 3ch with a sl st, turn.

JOINED YOKE R4

Note: When the number of trebles given is 0, miss this sp.

Back: 3ch, 2tr in same sp, 3tr in each sp to sp before r-sp, 1 (0, 3, 3, 3, 3, 3, 3) tr in sp, 2tr in r-sp,

Sleeve: 3tr in each of next 19 (20, 19, 19, 19, 19, 20, 20) sps, 2tr in r-sp,

Front: 1 (0, 3, 3, 3, 3, 3, 3) tr in next sp, 3tr in each of next 20 (22, 22, 22, 24, 24, 26, 26) sps, 1 (0, 3, 3, 3, 3, 3, 3) tr in sp before r-sp, 2tr in r-sp,

Rep from * to ** for second sleeve.

Back: 1 (0, 3, 3, 3, 3, 3, 3) tr in next sp, 3tr in each sp to end, join to top of 3ch with a sl st, turn.

JOINED YOKE R5

3ch, 2tr in same sp, 3tr in each sp to r-sp (XS only: Miss last sp before r-sp), 2tr in r-sp, *3tr in each of next 20 (21, 20, 20, 20, 20, 21, 21) sps, 2tr in r-sp,** (XS only: Miss first sp after r-sp), 3tr in each of next 21 (23, 25, 25, 27, 27, 29, 29) sps, (XS only: Miss last sp before r-sp), 2tr in r-sp, rep from * to **, (XS only: Miss first sp after r-sp), 3tr in each sp to end, join to top of 3ch with a sl st, turn.

Sizes XS (S, M): Finish yoke here, secure with st marker and work from Join Underarms section. You will have 24 (25, 26) rows in total. 21 (23, 25) groups across front/back and 20 (21, 20) groups across each sleeve.

JOINED YOKE R6

3ch, 2tr in same sp, [3tr in each sp to r-sp, 2tr in r-sp] 4 times, 3tr in each sp to end, join to top of 3ch with a sl st, turn. You will have x (x, x, 26, 28, 28, 30, 30) groups across front/back, and x (x, x, 21, 21, 21, 22, 22) groups across each sleeve.

Sizes L (XL): Finish yoke here, secure with st marker and work from Join Underarms section. You will have 27 (28) rows in total.

JOINED YOKE R7

Rep previous row. You will have x (x, x, x, x, 29, 31, 31) groups across front/back, and x (x, x, x, x, 22, 23, 23) groups across each sleeve.

Sizes 2XL (3XL): Finish yoke here, secure with st marker and work from Join Underarms section. You will have 29 (30) rows in total.

JOINED YOKE R8

Rep joined yoke R6. You will have 32 groups across front/back, and 24 groups across each sleeve. finish yoke here, secure with st marker and work from Join Underarms section. You will have 31 rows in total.

JOIN UNDERARMS

Fold your yoke in half across the shoulders. Join the two left corners together and the two right corners together as follows: Using a separate ball of yarn, attach yarn to sp between the 2tr sts of the r-sp on front left corner. 6 (6, 9, 12, 15, 18, 21, 24) ch, sl st to sp between the 2tr sts of the r-sp on back left corner, fasten off. Repeat with right corners.

Body R1: Working from centre back, remove st marker, 3ch, 2tr in same sp, 3tr in each sp to r-sp, *miss r-sp and all sleeve sts and work across underarm ch as follows: miss 1ch, 3tr in next ch, [miss 2ch, 3tr in next ch] 1 (1, 2, 3, 4, 5, 6, 7) times, miss 1ch and r-sp,** 3tr in each sp across front to r-sp, rep from * to **, 3tr in each sp to end, join to top of 3ch with a sl st, turn. You will have 48 (52, 58, 62, 68, 72, 78, 82) 3tr groups around the body (B).

Body R2: 3ch, 2tr in same sp, 3tr in each sp to end, join to top of 3ch with a sl st, turn.

Rep Body R2 until you have 59 (61, 63, 65, 67, 69, 71, 73) rows from start of yoke.

Decrease round: 3ch, 2tr in sp, (1tr, tr2tog) in next sp, [3tr in next sp, (1tr, tr2tog) in next sp] to end, join to top of 3ch with a sl st.

Hem Edging

R1: With rs facing (turn if necessary), 1ch, 1dc into each st to end, join to top of first dc with a sl st, do not turn.

R2: 1ch, 1dc into each st to end, join to top of first dc with a sl st, fasten off.

B

XS YOKE AFTER BODY R1

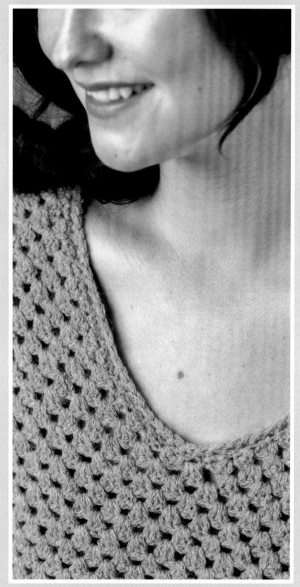

Neck Edging

R1: With rs facing, attach yarn to fdc st at centre of back neck. 1ch, 1dc into each st to back left raglan corner, dc2tog across st at corner and next st, 1dc in each st across left shoulder to front left raglan corner, dc evenly down left front V edge to centre (work 5dc across 2 rows), 1dc in 1ch at base of V, dc evenly up right front V edge to right front raglan corner, 1dc in each st across right shoulder to back right raglan corner, dc2tog across st at corner and next st, 1dc in each st to end, join to top of first dc with a sl st, do not turn.

R2: 1ch, 1dc in each st to back left raglan corner, dc2tog across st at corner and next st, 1dc in each st to back right raglan corner, dc2tog across st at corner and next st, 1dc in each st to end, join to top of first dc with a sl st, fasten off.

Sleeves

Note: Depending on whether your yoke finished on a rs or a ws round, and whether you are on your left or your right sleeve, you may work down to and across the underarm first and work around most of the upper armhole second, or vice versa. Either way, work around the upper armhole and across the underarm as explained in R1.

R1: With the ws of the sts around upper armhole section facing you, attach yarn into any sp on the upper armhole section, on the back of the jumper (C), 3ch, 2tr in same sp, 3tr in each sp around upper armhole until you reach the underarm, miss 2tr group and sp after it, 3tr in each of the 1 (1, 2, 3, 4, 5, 6, 7) sps between underarm groups already there, miss sp before 2tr group and 2tr group on other side of underarm, 3tr in each sp to end, join to top of 3ch with a sl st turn. 21 (23, 23, 25, 26, 28, 30, 32) groups.

Sizes M (XL, 3XL) only: Place a stitch marker in sp between first (second, third) and second (third, fourth) group across underarm to mark centre.

Sizes XS (S, L, 2XL, 4XL) only: Place a stitch marker in first (first, second, third, fourth) group across underarm to mark centre.

R2: 3ch, 2tr in same sp, 3tr in each sp to end, join with a sl st to top of 3ch, turn.

Rep R2 2 (0, 1, 0, 1, 0, 1, 0) times. You will have 4 (2, 3, 2, 3, 2, 3, 2) rows.

Decrease R1: 3ch, 2tr in same sp, 3tr in each sp until you reach the sp directly in line with the st marker, work 2tr in this sp, 3tr in each sp to end, join with a sl st to top of 3ch, turn.

Decrease R2: 3ch, 2tr in same sp, 3tr in each sp until you reach the sp before the 2tr group, miss the sp before the 2tr group, 3tr in between the 2tr of the group, miss the sp after the 2tr group, 3tr in each sp to end, join with a sl st to top of 3ch, turn. Work your size as follows:

[Rep R2 3 times, followed by decrease R1 and 2] 7 (7, 8, 6, 6, 4, 2, 0) times. You will have 41 (39, 45, 34, 35, 24, 15, 4) rows and 13 (15, 14, 18, 19, 23, 27, 31) groups.

C

Start R1 on back of armhole.

Sizes S and L–4XL only: [Rep R2 once, followed by decrease R1 and 2] x (2, x, 4, 4, 8, 11, 15) times.

You will have 13 (13, 14, 14, 15, 15, 16, 16) groups and 41 (45, 45, 46, 47, 48, 48, 49) rounds.

All sizes: Rep R2 a further 8 (4, 5, 5, 4, 4, 4, 4) times, or until sleeve reaches wrist. Rep R2 a further 7 times for cuff turn up.

Cuff Edging

R1: With rs facing (turn if necessary), 1ch, 1dc into each st to end, join to top of first dc with a sl st, do not turn.

R2: 1ch, 1dc into each st to end, join to top of first dc with a sl st, fasten off.

Repeat for second sleeve. Fold edging stitches up by 1cm (⅜in) on outside of jumper, then fold a further 7 rows up on outside of jumper (edging sts should be tucked in and not visible) to create the cuff turn up.

Weave in all ends and block to given dimensions.

TIP

IF YOU FIND YOUR GARMENT STARTS TO PILL, INVEST IN A DE-PILLING TOOL AND GIVE IT A SHAVE TO REMOVE THOSE BOBBLES.

Geometric Cowl

This geometric patterned cowl is a great way to practise changing colours in granny stitch. Make sure you read the Taking It Further section and you'll be effortlessly switching colours in no time.

YOU WILL NEED

Hook: 4mm (G/6)

Scissors

Yarn needle

Yarn: Viking Garn Alpaca Storm. 40% Alpaca superfine, 40% Merino, 20% Nylon, 50g (1¾oz) = 133m (145½yd), in the following shades:

- Yarn A: 545
- Yarn B: 515
- Yarn C: 564

PATTERN NOTES

Yarn weight: DK

Tension: 5 x 3tr groups and 11 rows = 10cm (4in)

Geometric Cowl Schematic

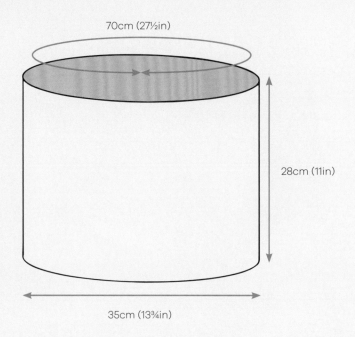

70cm (27½in)

28cm (11in)

35cm (13¾in)

Yardage and Sizing

YARN QUANTITIES:

Yarn A	61g (2⅛oz)/ 163m (178¼yd)
Yarn B	33g (1⅛oz)/ 88m (96¼yd)
Yarn C	41g (1½oz)/ 110m (120⅜yd)

SIZING CHART:

Width	35cm (13¾in)
Circumference	70cm (27½in)
Height	28cm (11in)

Cowl

Set up round: Using yarn A, 105 fdc, join to first st with a sl st to form a circle.

Alternatively, 105ch, join to first ch with a sl st to form a circle. 1ch, 1dc into each st to end. 105sts.

In the next round you are going to work groups of 3tr over the dc sts and into the bottom ch.

R1: 3ch (counts as first tr) 2tr in first ch, (miss 2 chs, 3tr in next ch) 34 times, miss 2 chs, join to top of 3ch with a sl st, turn. 35 3tr groups.

R2: 3ch, 2tr in same sp, 3tr in next sp ,*3tr in next sp in yarn B, 3tr in next 4 sps in yarn A**, Repeat from * to ** 5 times, 3tr in next sp in yarn B, 3tr in last 2 sps in yarn A, join to top of 3ch with a sl st, turn.

R3: Using yarn A, 3ch, 2tr in same sp, 3tr in next sp, *3tr in each of the next 2 sps in yarn B, 3tr in each of the next 3 sps in yarn A**, rep from * to ** 5 times, 3tr in each of the next 2 sps in yarn B, 3tr in last sp in yarn A, join to top of 3ch with a sl st, turn.

R4: Using yarn A, 3ch, 2tr in same sp, *3tr in each of next 3 sps in yarn B, 3tr in each of next 2 sps in yarn A**, rep from * to ** 5 times, 3tr in next 3 sps in yarn B, 3tr in last sp in yarn A, join to top of 3ch with a sl st, turn.

R5: Using yarn A, 3ch, 2tr in same sp, *3tr in each of next 4 sps in yarn B, 3tr in next sp in yarn A**, rep from * to ** 5 times, 3tr in each of next 4 sps in yarn B, join to top of 3ch with a sl st, turn.

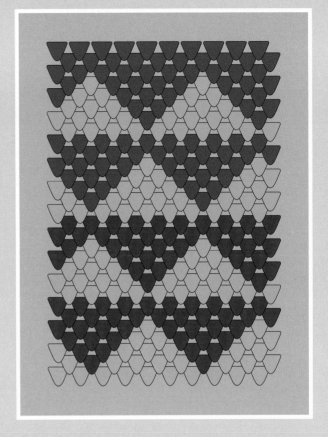

TIP

TO CREATE DIFFERENT EFFECTS, TRY WORKING THE COWL IN TWO COLOURS ONLY, OR WORKING THE YARN B AND C SECTIONS IN FOUR DIFFERENT COLOURS INSTEAD OF TWO.

R6: Using yarn B, 3ch, 2tr in same sp, 3tr in each sp to end, join to top of 3ch with a sl st, turn.

R7: Rep R6, working last yo of last st in yarn A. Join to top of 3ch with a sl st in yarn A, turn.

R8: Using yarn A, 3ch, 2tr in same sp, 3tr in each sp to end, working last yo of last st in yarn B. Join to top of 3ch with a sl st in yarn B, turn.

R9: Using yarn B, 3ch, 2tr in same sp, *3tr in each of next 4 sps in yarn A, 3tr in next sp in yarn B**, rep from * to ** 5 times, 3tr in each of last 4 sps in yarn A, working last yo of last st in yarn B. Join to top of 3ch with a sl st in yarn B, turn.

R10: Using yarn B, 3ch, 2tr in same sp, *3tr in each of next 3 sps in yarn A, 3tr in each of next 2 sps in yarn B**, rep from * to ** 5 times, 3tr in each of next 3 sps in yarn A, 3tr in last sp in yarn B, join to top of 3ch with a sl st, turn.

R11: Using yarn B, 3ch, 2tr in same sp, 3tr in next sp, *3tr in next 2 sps in yarn A, 3tr in each of next 3 sps in yarn B, rep from * to ** 5 times, 3tr in next 2 sps in yarn A, 3tr in last sp in yarn B, join to top of 3ch with a sl st, turn.

R12: Using yarn B, 3ch, 2tr in same sp, 3tr in next sp, *3tr in next sp in yarn A, 3tr in each of next 4 sps in yarn B**, rep from * to ** 5 times, 3tr in next sp in yarn A, 3tr in last 2 sps in yarn B, join to top of 3ch with a sl st, turn.

R13: Using yarn B, 3ch, 2tr in same sp, 3tr in each sp to end, join to top of 3ch with a sl st, turn.

R14: Rep R13. Fasten off yarn B.

R15: Attach yarn A into sl st sp, 3ch, 2tr in same sp, 3tr in each sp to end, join to top of 3ch with a sl st, turn.

Rep R2–R14 replacing yarn B with yarn C. Fasten off yarn A after R12. Do not fasten off yarn C after R14.

Rep R13 once more, do not turn. 29 rows.

Finishing row: 1ch, 1dc in each st to end. Join to top of first dc with a sl st. Fasten off.

On bottom edge, attach yarn A in the first ch. 1ch, 1dc in each ch to end Join to top of first dc with a sl st. Fasten off and weave in all ends.

Boho Scarf

This statement scarf will add a bohemian feel to any outfit and the size can be easily customized. Try it with or without tassels, or add pom-poms or fringing to change up the look.

✧ YOU WILL NEED

Hook: 4mm (G/6), 4.5mm (7) for the slip stitches

Scissors

Yarn needle

Small square of cardboard for making tassels

Yarn: Hobbii Kind Feather. 100% Acrylic, 100g (3½oz) = 235m (257yd) in the following shades:

- Yarn A: Light Gray 27
- Yarn B: Petrol Blue 18
- Yarn C: Camel 23
- Yarn D: Pink 11

✧ PATTERN NOTES

Yarn weight: DK

Tension: 4.5 x 3tr groups and 9 rows = 10cm (4in)

To shorten or increase length, remove/add multiples of six 3tr groups in row 1 and 18 fdc from the set up row. For every six groups you remove/add, the scarf will be 13cm (5in) shorter/longer.

See the notes on changing colour in Taking It Further.

Boho Scarf Schematic

29cm
(11½in)

215cm (84½in) not including tassels

Yardage and Sizing

YARN QUANTITIES:

Yarn A	295g (10½oz)/ 693m (758yd)
Yarn B	89g (3¼oz)/ 209m (228½yd)
Yarn C	44g (1½oz)/ 103m (112½yd)
Yarn D	15g (½oz)/35m (38¼yd)

SIZING CHART:

Length	215cm (84½in)
Width	29cm (11½in)

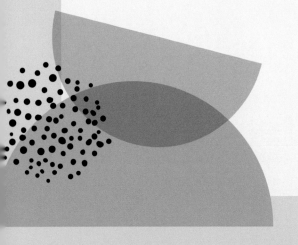

Scarf

Set up row: Using yarn A and a 4mm (G/6) hook, 293 fdc.

Alternatively, 294ch. 1dc in second ch from hook, 1dc in each ch to end, turn. 293 sts.

In the next round you are going to work groups of 3tr over the dc sts and into the bottom ch.

R1 (rs): 3ch (counts as first tr here and throughout), miss 1 ch, 3tr in next ch, *miss 2 chs, 3tr in next ch, rep from * to last 2 chs, miss 1 ch, 1tr in last ch, turn. 97 3tr groups.

R2: 3ch, 1tr in same sp, 3tr in next sp, using yarn B, 3tr in next sp, *using yarn A, 3tr in each of next 2 sps, using yarn B, 3tr in next sp, rep from * to last 2 sps, using yarn A, 3tr in next sp, 1tr in last sp, 1tr in top of 3ch, turn. 96 3tr groups.

R3: 3ch, 3tr in next sp, *using yarn B, 3tr in each of next 2 sps, using yarn A, 3tr in next sp, rep from * to end, 1tr in top of 3ch, turn.

R4: Using yarn A, 3ch, 1tr in same sp, (drop yarn A but do not fasten off or carry along row), using yarn B, 3tr in next sp, using yarn C, 3tr in next sp, *using yarn B, 3tr in each of next 2 sps, using yarn C, 3tr in next sp, rep from * to last 2 sps. Using yarn B, 3tr in next sp, attach a small amount of yarn A and 1tr in last sp, 1tr in top of 3ch, working last yo in yarn B, turn. Fasten off yarn A.

R5: Using yarn B, 3ch, 3tr in next sp, *using yarn C, 3tr in each of next 2 sps, using yarn B, 3tr in next sp, rep from * to end, 1tr in top of 3ch, picking up yarn A to work the last yo, turn. Fasten off yarns B and C.

R6: Using yarn A, 3ch, 1tr in same sp, 3tr in next sp, using yarn D, 3tr in next sp, *using yarn A, 3tr in each of next 2 sps, using yarn D, 3tr in next sp, rep from * to last 2 sps, using yarn A, 3tr in next sp, 1tr in last sp, 1tr in top of 3ch, turn. Fasten off yarn D.

R7: Using yarn A, 3ch, 3tr in each sp to end, 1tr in top of 3ch, turn.

R8: 3ch, 1tr in same sp, 3tr in each sp to last sp, 1tr in last sp, 1tr in top of 3ch, turn.

R9: Rep R7. Do not fasten off yarn A.

R10–R11: Rep R8 and R7 using yarn B. Fasten off yarn B.

R12–R14: Rep R8, R7, R8: using yarn A, working last yo in yarn D. Do not fasten off yarn A.

R15: Using yarn D, 3ch, 3tr in next sp, *using yarn C, 3tr in next sp, using yarn D, 3tr in next sp, rep from * to last sp, still using yarn D, 1tr in top of 3ch, working last yo in yarn C, turn. Fasten off yarn D.

R16: Using yarn C, rep R8. Fasten off yarn C.

Rows 7 and 8 form pattern. Using yarn A, rep pattern four times, 24 rows in total. Do not fasten off.

Note: You can make the scarf thinner by working 22 or 20 rows.

EDGE TRIM

Work with rs facing.

R1: 1ch, 1dc in each st down length of scarf edge. After last st, change to 4.5mm (7) hook, 1ch, sl st evenly across end of scarf (working 5 sl st per 2 rows), sl st into first st of opposite side.

R2: Change to 4mm (G/6) hook, turn, 1ch, 1dc into each sl st (under both loops), to end, turn.

R3: 1ch, 1dc in each st to end.

Rep R1, R2 and R3 on opposite side of scarf. Join to top of first st with a sl st. Fasten off.

Weave in all ends and block to given dimensions.

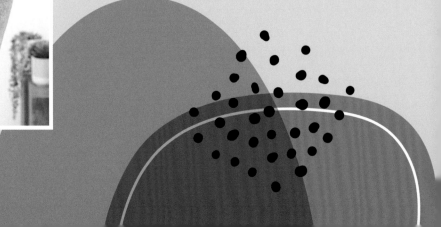

MAKING THE TASSELS

Make four tassels in yarn B. Cut a piece of card approx 11cm (4¼in) long, and wind the yarn around the card 50 times (A). Cut a 40cm (15¾in) long piece of yarn and, using a yarn needle, thread it under the top of the tassel, and tie it in a knot to secure (B). Carefully slide the tassel off the card (C) and then tightly wrap yarn around the tassel 10 times, approximately 1.5cm (½in) from the top. Tie in a knot to secure and, using a yarn needle, insert the yarn ends under the yarn you have just wound around and down into the tassel to hide them (D).

Snip through the looped strands at the bottom of the tassel with scissors. Then hold the ends of your tassel together and trim with scissors to neaten the ends (E).

Thread one of the two ends securing the top of the tassel onto the yarn needle and pass the needle through the scarf, from the front to the back about 1cm (⅜in) in from a corner. Hold in place, while threading up the other end and doing the same, but 5mm (⅛in) away from the first piece, and then tie the two ends together on the back of the scarf in a knot. Thread the needle with the yarn ends and insert them back through the scarf into the top of the tassel and down inside it, to hide them. Repeat on all four corners.

TIP

RUN YOUR TASSEL THROUGH HAIR STRAIGHTENERS ON THE COOLEST SETTING FOR SUPER-STRAIGHT STRANDS BEFORE TRIMMING YOUR ENDS.

A   B   C   D   E

Colour Pop Mittens

Made with the softest Merino yarn, these fun granny stripe mittens feature bright pops of colour and will keep your hands snug and stylish all winter long.

◇ YOU WILL NEED

Hook: 4mm (G/6)

Scissors

Yarn needle

Yarn: Scheepjes Merino Soft. 50% Superwash Merino wool, 25% Microfibre, 25% Acrylic, 50g (1¾oz) = 105m (115yd), in the following shades:

- Yarn A: Ansingh 643
- Yarn B: Munch 620
- Yarn C: Matisse 635
- Yarn D: Raphael 602

◇ PATTERN NOTES

Yarn weight: DK

Tension: 5 x 3tr groups and 11 rows = 10cm (4in)

Colour Pop Mittens Schematic

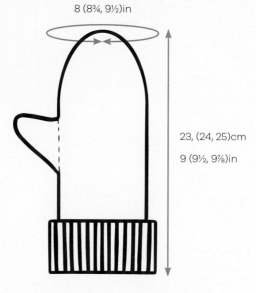

20 (22, 24)cm

8 (8¾, 9½)in

23, (24, 25)cm

9 (9½, 9⅞)in

Yardage and Sizing

SIZING CHART:

	S	M	L
Hand circumference	18.5-20cm (7¼–8in)	20.5-22cm (8⅛– 8¾in)	22.5-24cm (8⅞–9½in)
Mitten circumference	20cm (8in)	22cm (8¾in)	24cm (9½in)
Mitten length	23cm (9in)	24cm (9½in)	25cm (9⅞in)

YARN QUANTITIES:

	S	M	L
Yarn A	80g (3oz)/168m (183¾yd)	90g (3¼oz)/189m (206½yd)	106g (3¾oz)/223m (243⅞yd)
Yarn B	12g (⅜oz)/25m (27⅜yd)	12g (⅜oz)/25m (27⅜yd)	14g (½oz)/30m (33yd)
Yarn C	12g (⅜oz)/25m (27⅜yd)	12g (⅜oz)/25m (27⅜yd)	14g (½oz)/30m (33yd)
Yarn D	12g (⅜oz)/25m (27⅜yd)	12g (⅜oz)/25m (27⅜yd)	14g (½oz)/30m (33yd)

Ribbed Cuff

Using yarn A, 24 (26, 28) ch.

R1: 1dc in second ch from hook (1 missed ch does not count as stitch) and in each ch to end. Turn. 23 (25, 27) sts.

R2: 1ch (does not count as st) 1dc blo in each st to end. Turn. 23 (25, 27) sts. Your cuff should measure 10 (11, 12)cm (4 [4⅜, 4¾]in) wide. If it does not, then reduce/increase the amount of sts to get the correct width.

Rep R2 until you have 40 (44, 48) rows. Bring both ends of your cuff together and line up. Sl st through both sides all the way up the width of the cuff to create a seam.

Main Mitten Body

Set up round 1: With the seam facing out, 1ch and work 30 (33, 36) dc evenly around the top of your cuff. To do this evenly, work 3dc across the top of every 4 rows, join to top of first dc with a sl st. Do not turn.

Set up round 2: 2ch, miss 1 st, [1dc in each of next 2 sts, 1ch, miss next st] 9 (10, 11) times, 1 dc in each of the last 2 sts, sl st into st below 2ch sp at start of previous row, do not turn.

In the next round, you are going to work your groups of 3tr over the 1ch sp and into the top of the dc from set up round 1.

R1: 3ch, 2tr in top of dc in row below current row, [miss 2 sts, 3tr in top of dc from row below current row] 9 (10, 11) times. Join to top of 3ch with a sl st, turn. 10 (11, 12) 3tr groups.

R2: 3ch, 2tr in same sp, 3tr in each sp to end, join to top of 3ch with a sl st, turn.

R3: Attach yarn B in sp joined with a sl st, 3ch, 2tr in same sp, 3tr in each sp to end, join to top of 3ch with a sl st, turn.

R4: Rep R2

R5 and R6: Using yarn A, rep R2.

START THUMBHOLE

R7: Attach yarn C in sp joined with a sl st, 3ch, 1tr in same sp, 3tr in next 9 (10, 11) sps, 2tr in same sp as 3ch and 1tr, do not join, turn.

R8: 3ch, 3tr in next 10 (11, 12) sps, 1tr in top of 3ch, do not join, turn.

R9: Using yarn A, 3ch, 1tr in same sp, 3tr in next 9 (10, 11) sps, 1tr in last sp, 1tr in top of 3ch, do not join, turn.

R10: 3ch, 3tr in next 10 (11, 12) sps, 1tr in top of 3ch, do not join, turn.

R11 and R12: Rep R9 and R10 using yarn D. At the end of R12, join to top of 3ch with a sl st, turn.

R13: Attach yarn A in sp between last 1tr and 3tr group, 2ch, 1tr in same sp, (counts as tr2tog), 3tr in next 9 (10, 11) sps, tr2tog in last sp, join to top of first tr2tog with a sl st, turn.

R14: Sl st into next sp, 3ch, 2tr in same sp, 3tr in next 9 (10, 11) sps, join to top of 3ch with a sl st, turn.

Rep R14. 1 (2, 3) times. 15 (16, 17) rows.

DECREASE SECTION

Note: Try to work a little bit tighter from this point on, to bring your treble groups together.

R1: 3ch, 2tr in same sp, 3tr in next sp, (1tr, tr2tog) in next sp, [3tr in next 2 sps, (1tr, tr2tog) in next sp] 2 (2, 3) times. Size M only: 3tr in next sp. Sizes S and M only: (1tr, tr2tog) in next sp, join to top of 3ch with a sl st, turn.

R2: 3ch, 2tr in same sp, [(1tr, t2tog) in next sp, 3tr in next sp] 4 (4, 5) times, (1tr, tr2tog) in next sp. Size M only: (1tr, tr2tog) in last sp, join to top of 3ch with a sl st, turn.

R3: 3ch, 2tr in same sp, [(1tr, t2tog) in next 2 sps, 3tr in next sp)] 3 times: Sizes M and (L) only: (1tr, tr2tog) in last 1 (2) sps, join to top of 3ch with a sl st, turn.

R4: 3ch, tr2tog in same sp, (1tr, t2tog) in each sp to end, join to top of 3ch with a sl st, turn.

R5: 2ch (counts as first htr), 1htr in same sp, 2htr in each sp to end, join to top of 2ch with a sl st, turn. 20 (22, 24) sts.

R6: [dc2tog across next 2 sts] 10 (11, 12) times, join to top of first dc with a sl st. 10 (11, 12) sts.

R7: [dc2tog across next 2 sts] 5 (5, 6) times: Size M only: 1dc in last st, join to top of first dc with a sl st, turn. 3 sts.

Cut yarn leaving 15cm (6in) remaining. Thread the end through a yarn needle, weave in and out though the top of the last round of sts and pull tight to gather the top. Knot yarn through the last st to secure.

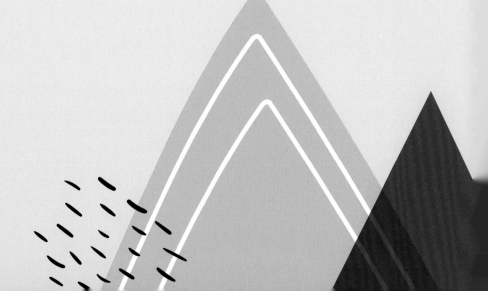

THUMB

R1: Attach yarn A to base of thumbhole between two 2tr groups. 1ch, work 24 dc around thumbhole. To do this evenly, work 2 dc per row. Join to top of first dc with a sl st, turn. 24 sts.

R2: 1ch, [dc2tog over next 2 sts, 1dc in each of next 10 sts] 2 times, join to top of first dc with a sl st, turn. 22 sts.

R3: 1ch, [dc2tog over next 2 sts, 1dc in each of next 9 sts] 2 times, join to top of first dc with a sl st, turn. 20 sts.

R4: 1ch, dc2tog over next 2 sts, 1dc in each of next 18 sts, join to top of first dc with a sl st, turn. 19 sts.

R5: 1ch, dc2tog over next 2 sts, 1dc in each of next 17 sts, join to top of first dc with a sl st, turn. 18 sts.

R6: 1ch, dc2tog over next 2 sts, 1dc in each of next 16 sts, join to top of first dc with a sl st, turn. 17 sts.

R7: 1ch, dc2tog over next 2 sts, 1dc in each of next 15 sts, join to top of first dc with a sl st, turn. 16 sts.

R8: 1ch, dc2tog over next 2 sts, 1dc in each of next 14 sts, join to top of first dc with a sl st, turn. 15 sts.

R9: 1ch, 1dc in each of next 15 sts, join to top of first dc with a sl st, turn.

R10: Rep R9 once more. Further rows can be added here if needed.

R11: 1ch, dc2tog across next 14 sts, join to top of first dc with a sl st. 7 sts.

Cut yarn leaving 15cm (6in) remaining. Thread the end through a yarn needle, weave in and out though the top of the last round of sts and pull tight to gather the top. Knot yarn through the last st to secure. Weave in all ends. Make the second mitten in the same way.

Colour Pop Beanie

This granny stripe beanie will turn heads and keep you super toasty on your outdoor adventures. Pair with the matching mittens or make as a surprise gift for someone special.

YOU WILL NEED

Hook: 4mm (G/6)

Scissors

Yarn needle

6cm (2½in) diameter pom-pom maker

Yarn: Scheepjes Merino Soft. 50% Superwash Merino wool, 25% Microfibre, 25% Acrylic, 50g (1¾oz) = 105m (115yd), in the following shades:

- Yarn A: Ansingh 643
- Yarn B: Munch 620
- Yarn C: Matisse 635
- Yarn D: Raphael 602

PATTERN NOTES

Yarn weight: DK

Tension: 5 x 3tr groups and 11 rows = 10cm (4in)

Colour Pop Beanie Schematic

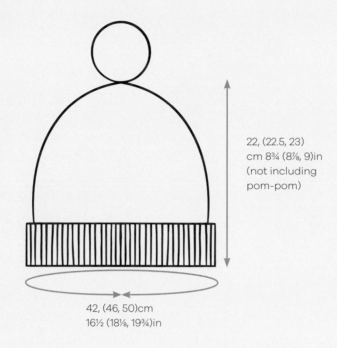

22, (22.5, 23)
cm 8¾ (8⅞, 9)in
(not including
pom-pom)

42, (46, 50)cm
16½ (18⅛, 19¾)in

Yardage and Sizing

SIZING CHART:

	S	M	L
Head circumference	51–54cm (20⅛–21¼in)	55–58cm (21¾–22⅞in)	59–62cm (23¼–24⅜in)
Hat circumference	42cm (16½in)	46cm (18⅛in)	50cm (19¾in)
Hat height	22cm (8¾in)	22.5cm (8⅞in)	23cm (9in)

YARN QUANTITIES:

	S	M	L
Yarn A	101g (3⅝oz)/212m (232yd)	111g (4oz)/233wm (255yd)	121g (4¼oz)/254m (277¾yd)
Yarn B	7g (¼oz)/15m (16½yd)	7g (¼oz)/15m (16½yd)	8g (¼oz)/17m (18¾yd)
Yarn C	7g (¼oz)/15m (16½yd)	7g (¼oz)/15m (16½yd)	8g (¼oz)/17m (18¾yd)
Yarn D	5g (⅛oz)/11m (12yd)	5g (⅛oz)/11m (12yd)	6g (⅛oz)/13m (14¼yd)

Ribbed Hat Band

Using yarn A 24 (26, 28) ch.

R1: 1dc in second ch from hook (1 missed ch does not count as stitch) and in each ch to end. Turn. 23 (25, 27) sts.

R2: 1ch (does not count as st) 1dc blo in each st to end. Turn. 23 (25, 27) sts. Your hat band should measure 10 (11, 12) cm (4 [4⅜, 4¾]in) wide. If it does not, then reduce/increase the amount of sts to get the correct width.

Rep R2 until you have 94 (103, 112) rows. Bring both ends of your hat band together and line up. Sl st through both sides all the way up the width of the band to create a seam.

Main Hat Body

Set up round 1: With the seam facing out, 1ch and work 63 (69, 75) dc evenly around the top of your hat band. To do this evenly, work 2dc across the top of every 3 rows until 1 row remains, work 1dc across last row, join to top of first dc with a sl st. Do not turn.

Set up round 2: 2ch, miss 1 st, [1dc in each of next 2 sts, 1ch, miss next st] 20 (22, 24) times, 1 dc in each of the last 2 sts, sl st into st below 2ch sp at start of previous row, do not turn.

In the next round, you are going to work your groups of 3tr over the 1ch sp and into the top of the dc from set up round 1.

R1: 3ch, 2tr in top of dc in row below current row, [miss 2 sts, 3tr in top of dc from row below current row] 20 (22, 24) times, miss 2 sts, join to top of 3ch with a sl st, turn. 21 (23, 25) 3tr groups.

R2: Attach yarn B in sp joined with a sl st, 3ch, 2tr in same sp, 3tr in each sp to end, join to top of 3ch with a sl st, turn.

R3: 3ch, 2tr in same sp, 3tr in each sp to end, join to top of 3ch with a sl st, turn.

R4 and R5: Using yarn A, rep R2 and R3.

R6 and R7: Using yarn C, rep R2 and R3.

R8: Using yarn A, rep R2.

START DECREASES FOR CROWN

R9: 3ch, 2tr in same sp, [1tr, tr2tog in next sp, 3tr in each of next 2 sps] 6 (7, 8) times. Size S only: (1tr, tr2tog) in next sp, 3tr in last sp. Size M only: (1tr, tr2tog) in last sp, join to top of 3ch with a sl st, turn.

Note: Try to work a little bit tighter from this point on, to bring your treble groups together.

R10: Attach yarn D in sp joined with a sl st, 3ch, 2tr in same sp, [1tr, tr2tog in next sp, 3tr in next sp] 10 (11, 12) times. Join to top of 3ch with a sl st, turn.

R11: 3ch, 2tr in same sp, [1tr, tr2tog in each of next 2 sps, 3tr in next sp] 6 (7, 8) times. Size S only: (1tr, tr2tog) in each of last 2 sps. Size M only: (1tr, tr2tog) in last sp. Join to top of 3ch with a sl st, turn.

R12: Attach yarn A in sp joined with a sl st, 3ch, tr2tog in same sp, [1tr, tr2tog in next sp] 20 (22, 24) times. Join to top of 3ch with a sl st, turn.

R13: 3ch, 1tr in same sp, 2tr in each sp to end. Join to top of 3ch with a sl st, turn.

R14: 3ch, 1tr in same sp, [tr2tog in next sp, 2tr in next sp] 10 (11, 12) times. Join to top of 3ch with a sl st, turn.

R15: 3ch, 1tr in same sp, [tr2tog in each of next 2 next sps, 2tr in next sp] 6 (7, 8) times. Size S only: 2tr in next sp, tr2tog in last sp. Size M only: tr2tog in last sp. Join to top of 3ch with a sl st, turn.

R16: 3ch, 1tr in same sp, tr2tog in each sp to end. Miss 3ch and join to top of first tr with a sl st, turn.

R17: 3ch in sp, 1tr in each sp to end. Join to top of 3ch with a sl st, turn. 21 (23, 25) sts.

R18: 2ch (counts as first htr), 1htr in each sp to end. Join to top of 2ch with a sl st, turn.

R19: 2ch, (counts as first htr), [htr2tog across next 2 sps] to end. Join to top of 2ch with a sl st. 11 (12, 13) sts.

Cut yarn leaving 15cm (6in) remaining. Thread the end through a yarn needle, weave in and out though the top of the last round of sts and pull tight to gather the top of the hat. Knot yarn through the last st to secure. Make a pom-pom using a 6cm (2½in) diameter pom-pom maker, trim and secure to top of hat. Weave in all ends.

TIP

FOR A DIFFERENT EFFECT, TRY USING AN OMBRE YARN, OR DO SOME STASHBUSTING BY USING A DIFFERENT COLOUR EVERY TWO ROWS.

Festive Jumper

Get in the Christmas spirit with this classic top-down jumper. With granny stripe details in seasonal colours and an easily customizable length, it will be a firm favourite this festive season.

◇ YOU WILL NEED

Hooks: 4mm (G/6), 5mm (H/8) for slip stitching on row 3b

Scissors

Yarn needle

4 x stitch markers

Yarn: Hobbi Kind Feather, 100% Acrylic, 100g (3½oz) = 235m (257yd), in the following shades:

- Yarn A: Hunter Green 20
- Yarn B: Light Gray 27
- Yarn C: Red 07

◇ PATTERN NOTES

Yarn weight: DK

Tension: 4.5 x 3tr groups and 10 rows = 10cm (4in)

Festive Jumper Schematic

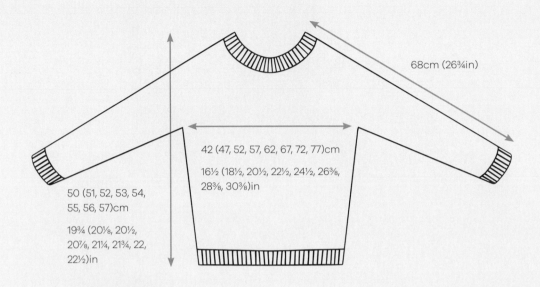

68cm (26¾in)

42 (47, 52, 57, 62, 67, 72, 77)cm

16½ (18½, 20½, 22½, 24½, 26⅜, 28⅜, 30⅜)in

50 (51, 52, 53, 54, 55, 56, 57)cm

19¾ (20⅛, 20½, 20⅞, 21¼, 21¾, 22, 22½)in

Yardage and Sizing

YARN QUANTITIES:

	XS	S	M	L	XL	2XL	3XL	4XL
Yarn A	433g (15¼oz)/ 1018m (1113¼yd)	457g (16⅛oz)/ 1074m (1174½yd)	488g (17¼oz)/ 1147m (1254⅜yd)	513g (18⅛oz)/ 1206m (1319yd)	544g (19¼oz)/ 1278m (1397⅝yd)	575g (20¼oz)/ 1351m (1477½yd)	634g (22⅜oz)/ 1490m (1629½yd)	652g (23oz)/ 1532m (1675⅝yd)
Yarn B	36g (1⅜oz) /85m (93yd)	39g (1⅜oz)/ 92m (100⅝yd)	40g (1⅜oz)/ 94m (102¾yd)	42g (1½oz)/ 99m (108¼yd)	43g (1½oz)/ 101m (110½yd	45g (1⅝oz)/ 106m (115⅞yd)	46g (1⅝oz)/ 108m (118⅛yd)	47g (1⅝oz)/ 110m (120¼yd)
Yarn C	48g (1¾oz)/ 113m (123⅝yd)	51g (1¾oz)/ 120m (131¼yd)	53g (1⅞oz)/ 125m (136¾yd)	55g (2oz)/ 129m (141⅛yd)	57g (2oz)/ 134m (146½yd)	59g (2⅛oz)/ 139m (152yd)	61g (2⅛oz)/ 143m (156⅜yd)	62g (2¼oz)/ 146m (159⅝yd)

SIZING CHART: 9CM (3½IN) POSITIVE EASE

	XS	S	M	L	XL	2XL	3XL	4XL
Bust	75cm (29½in)	85cm (33½in)	95cm (37⅜in)	105cm (41⅜in)	115cm (45¼in)	125cm (49¼in)	135cm (53⅛in)	145cm (57⅛in)
Garment circumference	84cm (33⅛in)	94cm (37in)	104cm (41in)	114cm (44⅞in)	124cm (48¾in)	134cm (52¾in)	144cm (56¾in)	154cm (60⅝in)
Garment width	42cm (16½in)	47cm (18½in)	52cm (20½in)	57cm (22½in)	62cm (24⅜in)	67cm (26⅜in)	72cm (28⅜in)	77cm (30⅜in)
Garment length	50cm (19¾in)	51cm (20⅛in)	52cm (20½in)	53cm (20⅞in)	54cm (21¼in)	55cm (21¾in)	56cm (22in)	57cm (22½in)
Sleeve length from neck	68cm (26¾in)	68cm (26¾in)	68cm (26¾in)	68cm (26¾in)	68cm (26¾in)	68cm (26¾in)	68cm (26¾in)	68cm (26¾in)

Construction

This jumper is worked in the round from the neck to the hem. The sleeves are worked from the yoke down and the length of the body and sleeves can easily be adjusted to fit.

Yoke

Set up round: Using yarn A and a 4mm (G/6) hook, 84 (84, 87, 87, 90, 90, 96, 96) fdc. Join with a sl st to top of first st.

On the next row you are going to work groups of 3tr over the dc sts and into the bottom ch.

R1 (rs): 3ch, 2tr in first ch, miss 2 chs, 4tr in next ch, [(miss 2 chs, 3tr in next ch) 3 times, miss 2 chs, 4tr in next ch] 6 (6, 6, 6, 5, 5, 7, 7) times. Sizes XL and 2XL only: (miss 2 chs, 3tr in next ch) 4 times, miss 2 chs, 4tr in next ch. ALL sizes: (miss 2 chs, 3tr in next ch) 2 (2, 3, 3, 3, 3, 2, 2) times, join to top of 3ch with a sl st. 28 (28, 29, 29, 30, 30, 32, 32) groups.

R2: Sl st across next 2 sts, sl st into sp, 3ch, 2tr in same sp, 3tr in sp between second and third tr of 4tr group, [3tr in next 4 sps, 3tr in sp between second and third tr of 4tr group] 6 (6, 6, 6, 5, 5, 7, 7) times. Sizes XL and 2XL only: 3tr in next 5 sps, 3tr in sp between second and third tr of 4tr group. ALL sizes: 3tr in next 3 (3, 4, 4, 4, 4, 3, 3) sps, join to top of 3ch with a sl st, fasten off. 35 (35, 36, 36, 37, 37, 40, 40) groups.

R3: Attach yarn B to sl st sp, 3ch, 2tr in sp, 3tr in each sp to end, join to top of 3ch with a sl st. Sl st blo across next 2 sts and place a st marker in last loop to secure.

R3b: Go back to previous sp and attach yarn C under front loop of first tr in last group of R3. Using a 5mm (H/8) hook, sl st flo across each tr st to end of round, sl st to first sl st and fasten off (A).

R4: Remove st marker from R3 and insert hook, using a 4mm (G/6) hook and yarn B, sl st into next sp, 3ch, 2tr in sp over sl sts, 3tr in each sp over sl sts to end, join to top of 3ch with a sl st, fasten off.

R5: Attach yarn A to sl st sp, 3ch, 2tr in same sp, 3tr in next 3 (3, 4, 4, 4, 4, 3, 3) sps, 4tr in next sp, [3tr in next 4 sps, 4tr in next sp] 6 (6, 6, 6, 5, 5, 7, 7) times. Sizes XL and 2XL only: 3tr in next 5 sps, 4tr in next sp. ALL sizes: Join to top of 3ch with a sl st.

R6: Sl st across next 2 sts, sl st into sp, 3ch, 2tr in sp, [3tr in next 3 (3, 4, 4, 4, 4, 3, 3) sps, 3tr in sp between second and third tr of 4tr group], [3tr in next 5 sps, 3tr in sp between second and third tr of 4tr group] 6 (6, 6, 6, 5, 5, 7, 7) times. Sizes XL and 2XL only: 3tr in next 6 sps, 3tr in sp between second and third tr of 4tr group. ALL sizes: 3tr in last sp, join to top of 3ch with a sl st, fasten off. 42 (42, 43, 43, 44, 44, 48, 48) groups.

R7: Attach yarn C to sl st sp, 3ch, 2tr in sp, 3tr in each sp to end, join to top of 3ch with a sl st, fasten off.

R8: Using yarn B, rep R7, fasten off.

R9: Using yarn C, rep R7, fasten off.

A

R10: Attach yarn A to sl st sp, 3ch, 2tr in same sp, 3tr in next 2 sps, 4tr in next sp, [3tr in next 5 sps, 4tr in next sp] 6 (6, 6, 6, 5, 5, 7, 7) times. Sizes XL and 2XL only: 3tr in next 6 sps, 4tr in next sp. ALL sizes: 3tr in next 2 (2, 3, 3, 3, 3, 2, 2) sps, join to top of 3ch with a sl st.

R11: Sl st across next 2 sts, sl st into sp, 3ch, 2tr in sp, 3tr in next 2 sps, 3tr in sp between second and third tr of 4tr group, [3tr in next 6 sps, 3tr in sp between second and third tr of 4tr group] 6 (6, 6, 6, 5, 5, 7, 7) times. Sizes XL and 2XL only: 3tr in next 7 sps, 3tr in sp between second and third tr of 4tr group. ALL sizes: 3tr in next 3 (3, 4, 4, 4, 4, 3, 3) sps, join to top of 3ch with a sl st, fasten off. 49 (49, 50, 50, 51, 51, 56, 56) groups.

R12, R13 and R14: Rep R7, R8 and R9.

R15: Attach yarn A to sl st sp, ch3, 2tr in same sp, 3tr in next 7 (5, 6, 5, 5, 3, 5, 5) sps, 4tr in next sp, [3tr in next 7 (6, 6, 5, 5, 5, 5, 5) sps, 4tr in next sp] 5 (6, 6, 6, 5, 6, 7, 7) times. Sizes L–4XL only: *3tr in next x (x, x, 6, 6, 4, 6, 6) sps, 4tr in next sp**. Size XL and 2XL only: Rep from * to **. ALL sizes: Join to top of 3ch with a sl st.

R16: Sl st across next 2 sts, sl st into sp, 3ch, 2tr in same sp, 3tr in next 7 (5, 6, 5, 5, 3, 5, 5) sps, 3tr in sp between second and third tr of 4tr group, [3tr in next 8 (7, 7, 6, 6, 6, 6, 6) sps, 3tr in sp between second and third tr of 4tr group] 5 (6, 6, 6, 5, 6, 7, 7) times. Sizes L–4XL only: *3tr in next x (x, x, 7, 7, 5, 7, 7) sps, 3tr in sp between second and third tr of 4tr group**. Sizes XL and 2XL only: Rep from * to **. ALL sizes: 3tr in last sp, join to top of 3ch with a sl st. Turn. 55 (56, 57, 58, 59, 60, 65, 65) groups.

From this point on, turn at the end of every round.

R17: 3ch, 2tr in same sp, 3tr in each sp to end, join to top of 3ch with a sl st, turn.

R18: 3ch, 2tr in sp, 3tr in next 4 (4, 3, 2, 2, 2, 2, 2) sps, 4tr in next sp, [3tr in next 10 (10, 7, 6, 6, 6, 6, 6) sps, 4tr in next sp] 3 (3, 5, 5, 4, 5, 6, 6) times, [3tr in next 10 (11, 8, 7, 7, 5, 7, 7) sps, 4tr in next sp] 1 (1, 1, 2, 3, 3, 2, 2) times, 3tr in last 5 (5, 3, 3, 3, 3, 3, 3) sps, join to top of 3ch with a sl st, turn.

R19: 3ch, 2tr in same sp, 3tr in each sp to end, working a 3tr group in the centre of each 4tr group as you pass them, join to top of 3ch with a sl st, turn. 60 (61, 64, 66, 67, 69, 74, 74) groups.

R20: 3ch, 2tr in same sp, 3tr in each sp to end, join to top of 3ch with a sl st, turn.

Size XS only: Rep R20 two more times, secure with st marker. End of yoke. Go to Dividing Yoke and Joining Underarms.

R21: 3ch, 2tr in sp, [3tr in next x (11, 9, 8, 8, 6, 7, 7) sps, 4tr in next sp] x (1, 3, 5, 4, 4, 8, 8) times, [3tr in next x (11, 10, 9, 9, 7, 8, 8) sps, 4tr in next sp] x (4, 3, 2, 3, 5, 1, 1) times, join to top of 3ch with a sl st, turn.

R22: 3ch, 2tr in same sp, 3tr in centre of the 4tr group, 3tr in each sp around, working a 3tr group in the centre of each 4tr group as you pass them, join to top of 3ch with a sl st, turn. x (66, 70, 73, 74, 78, 83, 83) groups.

R23: 3ch, 2tr in same sp, 3tr in each sp to end, join to top of 3ch with a sl st, turn.

Size S only: Secure with st marker. End of yoke. Go to Dividing Yoke and Joining Underarms.

Size M only: Rep R23 once. Secure with st marker. End of yoke. Go to Dividing Yoke and Joining Underarms.

R24: 3ch, 2tr in sp, 3tr in next x (x, x, 11, 8, 3, 4, 4) sps, 4tr in next sp, [3tr in next x (x, x, 23, 17, 9, 8, 8) sps, 4tr in next sp], x (x, x, 1, 2, 6, 7, 7) times, 3tr in next x (x, x, 23, 18, 8, 9, 9) sps, 4tr in next sp, 3tr in last x (x, x, 12, 9, 4, 4, 4) sps, join to top of 3ch with a sl st, turn.

R25: 3ch, 2tr in same sp, 3tr in each sp to end, working a 3tr group in the centre of each 4tr group as you pass them, join to top of 3ch with a sl st, turn. x (x, x, 76, 78, 86, 92, 92) groups.

Size L only: Secure with st marker. End of yoke. Go to Dividing Yoke and Joining Underarms.

R26: 3ch, 2tr in same sp, 3tr in each sp to end, join to top of 3ch with a sl st, turn.

Size XL only: Secure with st marker. End of yoke. Go to Dividing Yoke and Joining Underarms.

Sizes 2XL (3XL) only: Rep R26 1 (2) more times, secure with st marker. End of yoke. Go to Dividing Yoke and Joining Underarms.

R27: 3ch, 2tr in same sp, [3tr in next 10 sps, 4tr in next sp] 5 times, [3tr in next 11 sps, 4tr in next sp] 3 times, join to top of 3ch with a sl st, turn.

R28: 3ch, 2tr in same sp, 3tr in centre of the 4tr group, 3tr in each sp to end, working a 3tr group in the centre of each 4tr group as you pass them, join to top of ch3 with a sl st, turn. 100 groups.

R29: 3ch, 2tr in same sp, 3tr in each sp to end, join to top of 3ch with a sl st, secure with st marker. End of yoke. Go to Dividing Yoke and Joining Underarms.

DIVIDING YOKE AND JOINING UNDERARMS

From the sl st sp you just joined, count 9 (10, 11, 12, 12, 13, 14, 15) groups, place a stitch marker in sp after the last group. Count 13 (14, 14, 15, 15, 17, 18, 20) groups for the sleeve, place a marker, count 17 (19, 21, 23, 24, 26, 28, 30) groups for the front, place a marker, count 13 (14, 14, 15, 15, 17, 18, 20) groups for the second sleeve, place a marker. You will have 8 (9, 10, 11, 12, 13, 14, 15) groups remaining for the back (B).

You will now join the underarms together with chains. Attach a separate piece of yarn A to any sp with a marker and 3 (3, 6, 6, 9, 9, 12, 12) ch. Sl st to the sp with the marker on the other side of the sleeve. Fasten off. Do the same on the other side. Remove stitch markers (C).

Body

R1: Continuing from the centre back, remove marker, insert hook, and turn work so the ws of the sts in the prev row are facing you. 3ch, 2tr in same sp, 3tr in each sp until you reach the underarm ch, 3tr in the space holding the start of the chain, work across the chain as follows: *Miss 1 ch, 3tr in next ch, [miss 2 ch, 3tr in next ch] 0 (0, 1, 1, 2, 2, 3, 3) times, miss 1 ch, 3tr in the sp holding the end of the chain**, 3tr in each sp across the front until you reach the second underarm. Rep from * to **. 3tr in each sp across the back, join to top of 3ch with a sl st, turn. 38 (42, 48, 52, 56, 60, 66, 70) groups.

R2: 3ch, 2tr in same sp, 3tr in each sp to end, join with a sl st to top of 3ch, turn.

Rep R2 4 (4, 3, 3, 4, 4, 3, 3) more times.

Decrease R1: 3ch, 2tr in same sp, 3tr in each sp across back until you reach the underarm. *Locate the sp directly in line with the centre of the underarm and work 2tr in this sp (D)**, 3tr in each sp to next underarm, rep from * to **, 3tr in each sp to end, join with a sl st to top of 3ch, turn.

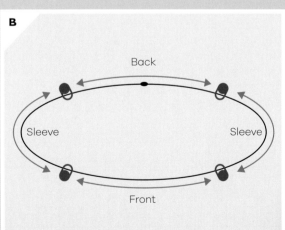

Decrease R2: 3ch, 2tr in same sp, 3tr in each sp across back until you reach the sp before the 2tr group, *miss the sp before the 2tr group, 3tr in between the 2tr of the group, miss the sp after the 2tr group (D)**, 3tr in each sp to next underarm, rep from * to **, 3tr in each sp to end, join with a sl st to top of 3ch, turn. 36 (40, 46, 50, 54, 58, 64, 68) groups.

Rep R2 5 (5, 7, 7, 5, 5, 7, 7) times.

Rep Decrease Rounds 1 and 2. 34 (38, 44, 48, 52, 56, 62, 66) groups.

Rep R2 2 (2, 1, 1, 2, 2, 1, 1) times.

Using yarn C, rep R2.

Using yarn B, rep R2.

Using yarn C, rep R2.

Using yarn A, rep R2.

Do not fasten off. You will have 21 rounds from yoke and 43 (44, 45, 46, 47, 48, 49, 50) rounds from neck.

Hem Rib

Start with the rs of body facing you. If you finished the body on a ws row you will need to turn.

R1: 8ch, 1dc in second ch from hook, (1ch missed does not count as stitch), 1dc in each of next 6 chs, sl st blo across top of 2 tr in first group along main body to anchor your rib to the body, turn. 7 sts.

R2: 1dc blo in next 7 sts, turn.

R3: 1ch, 1dc blo in next 7 sts, sl st blo across top of next 2 tr along edge, turn.

R2 and R3 form pattern. Rep pattern to end and seam edges together on ws using slip stitch.

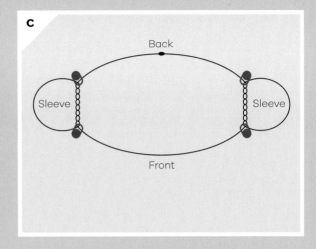

C

Back

Sleeve

Sleeve

Front

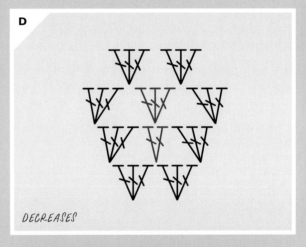

D

DECREASES

Sleeves

You will use the same method as as you did for the body to decrease down the sleeve. To lengthen or shorten sleeves, add or omit 2 rounds between each pair of decrease rounds as necessary.

Note: Depending on whether your yoke finished on a rs or a ws round, and whether you are on your left or your right sleeve, you may work down to and across the underarm first and work around most of the upper armhole second, or vice versa. Either way, work around the upper armhole and across the underarm as explained in R1.

R1: With the ws of the sts around upper armhole section facing you, attach yarn A into any sp on the upper armhole section, on the back of the jumper (E). 3ch, 2tr in same sp, 3tr in each sp around upper armhole until you reach the underarm, 3tr in each of the 2 (2, 3, 3, 4, 4, 5, 5) sps between underarm groups already there, 3tr in each sp to end, join to top of 3ch with a sl st, turn. 14 (15, 16, 17, 18, 20, 22, 24) groups.

Sizes XS and S only: Place a stitch marker in sp between first and second group across underarm to mark centre.

Sizes M and L only: Place a stitch marker in second group across underarm to mark centre.

Sizes XL and 2XL only: Place a stitch marker in sp between third and fourth group across underarm to mark centre.

Sizes 3XL and 4XL only: Place a stitch marker in third group across underarm to mark centre.

R2: 3ch, 2tr in same sp, 3tr in each sp to end, join with a sl st to top of 3ch, turn.

Rep R2 15 (15, 14, 14, 13, 7, 5, 0) times.

Decrease R1: 3ch, 2tr in same sp, 3tr in each sp until you reach the sp directly in line with the st marker, work 2tr in this sp, 3tr in each sp to end, join with a sl st to top of 3ch, turn.

Decrease R2: 3ch, 2tr in same sp, 3tr in each sp until you reach the sp before the 2tr group, miss the sp before the 2tr group, 3tr in between the 2tr of the group, miss the sp after the 2tr group, 3tr in each sp to end, join with a sl st to top of 3ch, turn. 13 (14, 15, 16, 17, 19, 21, 23) groups.

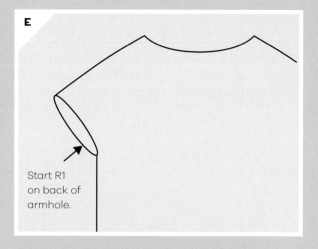

Start R1 on back of armhole.

Work your size as follows:

Size XS only: Rep R2 16 times in yarn A, then once in yarn C, once in yarn B and once in yarn C. 13 groups and 38 rounds. Go to final sleeve round.

Size S only: Rep R2 9 times, followed by decrease R1 and 2, rep R2 4 times in yarn A, then once in yarn C, once in yarn B and once in yarn C. 13 groups and 37 rounds. Go to final sleeve round.

Size M only: Rep R2 9 times, followed by decrease R1 and 2, rep R2 4 times in yarn A, then once in yarn C, once in yarn B and once in yarn C. 14 groups and 36 rounds. Go to final sleeve round.

Size L only: Rep R2 7 times, followed by decrease R1 and 2, rep R2 3 times, followed by decrease R1 and 2, rep R2 once in yarn C, once in yarn B and once in yarn C. 14 groups and 35 rounds. Go to final sleeve round.

Size XL only: [Rep R2 5 times, followed by decrease R1 and 2] twice, rep R2 once in yarn C, once in yarn B and once in yarn C. 15 groups and 34 rounds. Go to final sleeve round.

2XL only: [Rep R2 3 times, followed by decrease R1 and 2] 3 times, rep R2 3 times, rep decrease R1 in yarn A and decrease R2 in yarn C, rep R2 in yarn B, and once more in yarn C. 15 groups and 33 rounds. Go to final sleeve round.

Size 3XL only: [Rep R2 3 times, followed by decrease R1 and 2] 4 times, rep R2 in yarn C, rep decrease R1 in yarn B, followed by decrease R2 in yarn C. 16 groups and 32 rounds. Go to final sleeve round.

Size 4XL only: [Rep R2 3 times, followed by decrease R1 and 2] 3 times, [Rep R2, followed by decrease R1 and 2] 3 times, rep R2 in yarn C, rep decrease R1 in yarn B, followed by decrease R2 in yarn C. 16 groups and 31 rounds. Go to final sleeve round.

All sizes – final sleeve round: Using yarn A, 3ch, tr2tog in same sp, (1tr, tr2tog) in next sp 11 (11, 11, 11, 14, 14, 14, 14) times, 3tr in last 1 (1, 2, 2, 0, 0, 1, 1) sp(s), join with a sl st to top of 3ch. Do not turn or fasten off. 27 (27, 30, 30, 30, 30, 33, 33) sts.

Cuff Rib

Work as for the hem rib.

Work second sleeve in the same way.

Neck Rib

R1: With rs facing out, attach yarn A to ch at centre back. 8ch, 1dc in second ch from hook, (1ch missed does not count as stitch), 1dc in each of next 6 chs, sl st across next 3 ch along starting ch to anchor your rib to the body, turn. 7 sts.

R2: 1dc blo in next 7 sts, turn.

R3: 1ch, 1dc blo in next 7 sts, sl st blo across next 3 ch along starting ch, turn.

R2 and R3 form pattern. Rep pattern to end and seam edges together on ws using slip stitch.

Weave in all ends and block garment to given dimensions.

Crochet Techniques

These basic crochet stitch instructions cover all the techniques you'll need to create the projects in this book. Flip back to these pages whenever you need a reminder of how to work a stitch.

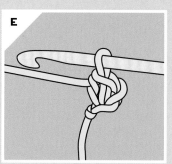

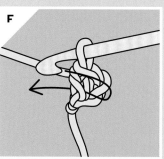

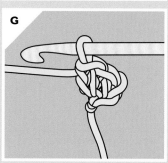

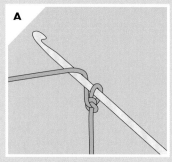

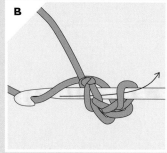

CHAIN (CH)

Yo, pull through the loop that is on your hook (A).

SLIP STITCH (SL ST)

Insert hook into stitch, yo, and pull through the stitch and the loop on your hook (B).

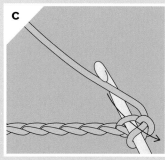

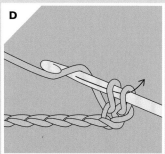

DOUBLE CROCHET (DC)

Insert hook into second loop from hook, *yo and pull through (C), yo and pull through both loops on your hook (D). Insert hook into next loop and rep from *.

FOUNDATION DOUBLE CROCHET (FDC)

2ch, insert your hook into the first ch (under both loops), yo and pull through, you will have 2 loops on your hook. Yo and pull through the first loop only. Yo and pull through both remaining loops on your hook. This creates the first stitch (E).

*Insert your hook under the two loops of the V on the top of your stitch, (the top is the side from which your working yarn is attached) (F).

Yo and pull through, you will have 2 loops on your hook. Yo and pull through the first loop only. Yo and pull through both remaining loops on your hook. This creates the second stitch (G).

Continue to repeat from * until you have worked the required amount of sts. If you are changing colour for the next row you should work the last yo in the new colour.

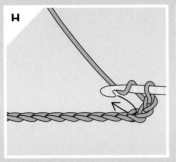
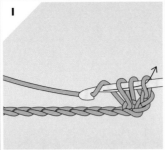
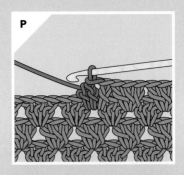

HALF TREBLE CROCHET (HTR)

Yo, and insert your hook into third chain from hook (H), *yo and pull through, yo and pull through all three loops on your hook (I). Insert hook into next chain, rep from *.

TREBLE CROCHET TWO TOGETHER (TR2TOG)

Yo and insert hook into sp, yo and pull through, yo and pull through the first two loops on your hook. Yo and insert hook into the same sp, yo and pull through, yo and pull through the first two loops on your hook, yo and pull through all three loops.

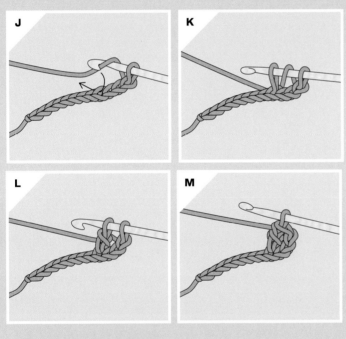

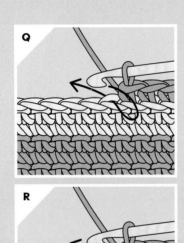

BACK OR FRONT LOOP ONLY (BLO, FLO)

When a pattern calls for you to work into the back or front loop of a stitch, you insert your hook into just one loop of the V on the top of the stitch. The back loop is the leg of the V that is furthest away from you and the front loop is the leg closest to you.

TREBLE CROCHET (TR)

Yo and insert hook into fourth chain from hook (J), *yo and pull through (K), yo and pull through the first two loops on your hook (L), yo and pull through the remaining two loops on your hook (M). Insert hook into next loop, rep from *.

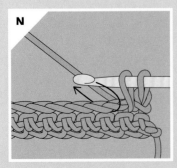
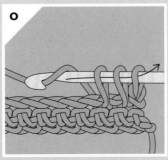

DOUBLE CROCHET TWO TOGETHER (DC2TOG)

Insert hook into stitch, yo and pull through (N), insert hook into next stitch, yo and pull through, yo and pull through all three loops on your hook (O).

Finishing Techniques

Some of the patterns in this book require sewing together. Whether it is a cardigan or a jumper, the method is the same. Sleeveless garments are quicker as there are usually only two panels. If you are new to making garments, try one of the sleeveless projects first.

BLOCKING

It is advisable to block your work to open up the stitches and even out the overall shape. Pin out your panels to the given dimensions on a foam mat and lay a damp cloth on top, or spray with a fine mist of water. Once your work is damp, remove the cloth and leave to dry.

You can also use an iron on the steam setting to block your work. Hover the iron over your work until it is damp. Ensure you cover all areas and do not touch your work with the iron as this can damage some fibres. Leave to dry.

SEWING A GARMENT TOGETHER

Top-down garments are worked in the round and require no seaming. Garments that are worked from the bottom up are mostly made in separate panels and sewn together at the end. The seams have the added benefit of adding structure and stability to the garment, meaning it's less likely to stretch or sag. To sew a garment together, first lay the front and back panels on top of each other with the right sides facing in. Pin and sew along the shoulder seams (A). I recommend using mattress stitch.

At the top of the sleeve, locate the central point (B). Place the sleeve inside the garment with the right sides facing each other and line up the central point with the shoulder seam (C). Pin the sleeve around the edge of the garment body and sew in place. Repeat on the other side with the second sleeve. Pin the remaining side seams together with the right sides facing in and sew together (D).

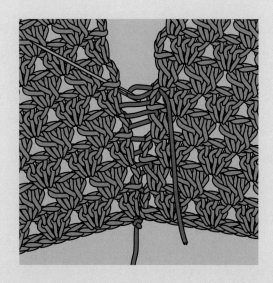

MATTRESS STITCH

Start at the bottom of your seam, with the ws facing you. Insert a threaded yarn needle into the first side. Then insert the yarn into the work on the other side, and then back into the first side, as if you were lacing up a pair of shoes.

If you are working along the top or bottom of a row of crochet you should match the stitches or chains to the stitches or chains on the other side, but if you are working up row edges, keep your stitches evenly spaced, and pinch your work into a slight seam with the rs facing one another. Then, insert your needle around 4mm (⅛in) from the edge on each stitch, to ensure that your work looks neat from the right side.

A

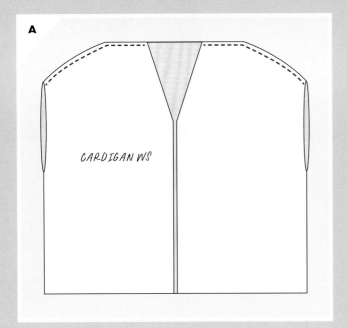

CARDIGAN WS

B

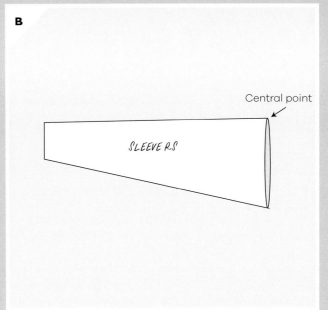

Central point

SLEEVE RS

C

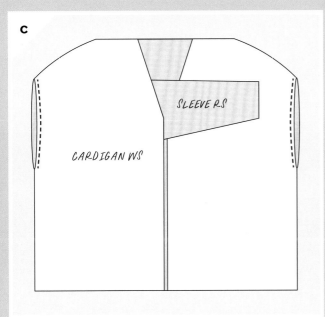

SLEEVE RS

CARDIGAN WS

D

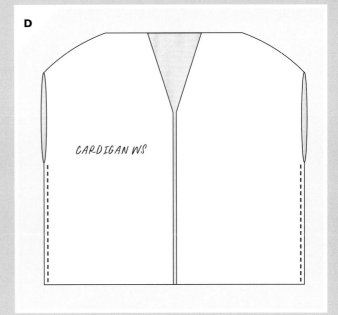

CARDIGAN WS

TIP

USE LONG PINS TO SECURE YOUR WORK AND USE A
MATCHING YARN COLOUR TO SEW UP YOUR SEAMS.

About the Author

Claudine lives by the sea in Cornwall with her husband and two children. She enjoys travelling, camping and exploring with her family as well as crochet, knitting and sewing. When not crocheting she can be found running on the Cornish coast path, sea dipping with her friends or hanging out at a skatepark with her husband and children.

Claudine has a background in fashion design and taught Textiles for 10 years, but now works as a freelance, independent crochet and knit designer. She runs workshops and has published designs in several craft and crochet magazines. She loves to make one-off items of clothing, is fond of bright colours, and never goes anywhere without a crochet project in her bag!

Claudine can be found on Instagram @iron_lamb and on her website www.ironlamb.co.uk

Contact: claudine@ironlamb.co.uk

Her designs can also be purchased from Etsy, Ravelry and Lovecrafts.

Thanks

First, thanks to Nick, Lola and Elmo, for bearing with me while I designed, made and wrote all of the patterns for this book. I know it was hard and I am so grateful for your love and support – I couldn't have done it without you. Thanks to my parents and in-laws for your constant encouragement, and my friends Eve and Kim for your moral support – I really appreciate it.

Thanks to the team at David and Charles for giving me this wonderful opportunity. Special thanks to Sarah and Jason for letting me be so involved in all the photoshoots and for being such fun to work with!

Thank you to my amazing pattern testers for giving up your time to help me perfect these designs. I couldn't have done this without you. Special thanks to Amy and Becca for going the extra mile to get things right.

Finally, thanks to you, my followers and customers, for sticking with me while I was absent from social media and for continuing to buy my work – I wouldn't be writing a book without your support and loyalty.

I hope you enjoy it xxx

Suppliers

Thank you to the companies who kindly supplied me with yarn for this book:

SCHEEPJES

www.scheepjes.com

HOBBII

www.hobbii.co.uk

SIRDAR

www.sirdar.com

Metric OR Imperial

All the projects in this book were made using metric measurements, and we have included imperial conversions for your convenience. The imperial conversions have all be rounded up to the nearest ⅛ or ¼ to ensure you have enough yarn. If you require more exact measurements, you might find it useful to use an online converter. When making the projects, always use either metric or imperial measurements, and never a combination of both.

Index

A DAVID AND CHARLES BOOK
© David and Charles, Ltd 2023

David and Charles is an imprint of David and Charles, Ltd
Suite A, Tourism House, Pynes Hill, Exeter, EX2 5WS

Text and Designs © Claudine Powley 2023
Layout and Photography © David and Charles, Ltd 2023

First published in the UK and USA in 2023

A catalogue record for this book is available from the British Library.

ISBN-13: 9781446309551 paperback
ISBN-13: 9781446382141 EPUB
ISBN-13: 9781446310342 PDF

This book has been printed on paper from approved suppliers and made from pulp from sustainable sources.

Printed in the UK by Pureprint for:
David and Charles, Ltd
Suite A, Tourism House, Pynes Hill, Exeter, EX2 5WS

10 9 8 7 6 5 4 3 2

Publishing Director: Ame Verso
Senior Commissioning Editor: Sarah Callard
Managing Editor: Jeni Chown
Editor: Jessica Cropper
Project Editor: Lindsay Kaubi
Technical Editor: Lauren Willis
Head of Design: Anna Wade
Designer: Sam Staddon
Pre-press Designer: Ali Stark
Illustrations: Kuo Kang Chen
Art Direction: Sarah Rowntree
Photography: Jason Jenkins
Production Manager: Beverley Richardson

David and Charles publishes high-quality books on a wide range of subjects. For more information visit www.davidandcharles.com.

Share your makes with us on social media using #dandcbooks and follow us on Facebook and Instagram by searching for @dandcbooks.

Layout of the digital edition of this book may vary depending on reader hardware and display settings.